THE REASONS FOR SEASONS

The Great Cosmic Megagalactic Trip
Without Moving from Your Chair

LINDA ALLISON

LITTLE, BROWN AND COMPANY
Boston   Toronto   London

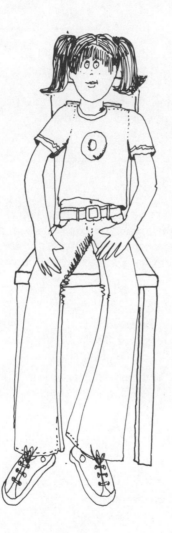

YOU THINK YOU ARE SITTING STILL.

The Brown Paper School is a series of small books about big
ideas, written and designed for kids and grownups together.
The series comes from a group of California teachers, writers
and artists who get together every now and then to work on
stuff for kids and to have a good time. They believe learning
only happens when it is wanted; that it can happen anywhere
and doesn't require fancy tools. This book and the others in
the series are dedicated to anyone who thinks so too.

Other books in The Brown Paper School series:
The I Hate Mathematics! Book, by Marilyn Burns
My Backyard History Book, by David Weitzman

The Brown Paper School series was edited and prepared for
publication at The Yolla Bolly Press in Covelo, California,
between September 1974 and January 1975. The series is
under the editorial direction of James Robertson. The staff
for the series is: Carolyn Robertson, Cindy Boatwright,
Colleen Carter, Sharon Miley, Sadako McInerney.

Published simultaneously in Canada by
Little, Brown & Company (Canada) Limited.
Printed in the United States of America. T 08/75

Library of Congress Cataloging in Publication Data

Allison, Linda.
  The reasons for seasons.

  (The brown paper school)
  SUMMARY: Stories to read, ideas to think about, and
things to make and do—all contributing to an understand-
ing of the seasons and their effect on the earth.
  1. Seasons—Juvenile literature. [1. Seasons]
I. Title.
QH81.A555   500.9   75-5930
  ISBN 0-316-03439-8   BP
  ISBN 0-316-03440-1 (pbk) BB

HC: 15 14 13 12 11 10 9 8 7
PB: 15 14 13 12 11 10

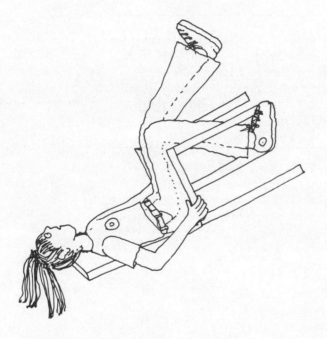

IN FACT YOU'RE NOT. IN FACT YOU
ARE ON THE GREAT COSMIC MEGA-
GALACTIC TRIP WITHOUT MOVING
FROM YOUR CHAIR. YOU ARE
TURNING A GIANT SOMERSAULT
EVERY TWENTY-FOUR HOURS
AND SPINNING AT ABOUT 1000
MILES PER HOUR.

AND CIRCLING THE SUN AT THE
RATE OF 6,500 MILES PER HOUR.

How To Use This Book

This is not a regular page 1 to page 128 book.
The pages are to be used in any order you like.
So if you want to, jump in at the middle — or
somewhere near the end.
However you fancy.

One hint:
Some times are better than other times for trying out
some sections of this book.
It's a book about seasons, and the projects are in seasonal order.
So you might try doing the Spring things in Spring time.
But some of the projects are good anytime.
(There's no time like now.)

Before you start:
Most everything in this book can be done by anybody,
anyplace, with whatever stuff is around the house.
Sometimes you might have to make a special trip to the dime store
or hardware store or supermarket.

The directions in this book are written in a general way.
That is because there is no such thing
as The Right Way to do anything.
If you don't like this way, try that way.
But mostly try it — and have a good time.

Now start.

YOU AND THE REST OF THE
SOLAR SYSTEM ARE TRAVELING
TOWARD THE STAR VEGA AT
12 MILES PER SECOND.

Contents

AND GYRATING AROUND THE
CENTER OF THE MILKY WAY
AT 150 MILES PER SECOND.

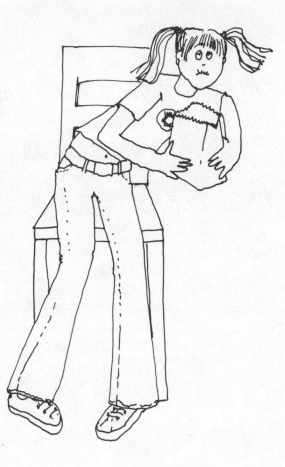

AND YOU THOUGHT YOU WERE SIT-
TING STILL! ALL THAT COMMO-
TION AND WE STILL HAVEN'T
TALKED ABOUT THE REASONS FOR
SEASONS.

THERE ARE TWO. ONE OF THEM IS
THE MOTION (THE PART ABOUT
CIRCLING AROUND THE SUN AT
6500 MILES PER HOUR). THE
OTHER ONE IS VERY PECULIAR.

The Other Reason

THE EARTH TRAVELS ROUND THE SUN FLOPPED OVER TO ONE SIDE, SO THE SUN'S LIGHT STRIKES IT IN A KIND OF LOPSIDED WAY.

SINCE EARLIEST TIMES, WE'VE BEEN WHEELING ROUND THE SUN AT THIS FUNNY TILT. WHAT'S EVEN MORE AMAZING ARE THE MILLIONS OF WAYS EARTH LIFE HAS LEARNED TO LIVE WITH THIS SILLY, SLANTED DANCE AND THE FITFUL FALL OF SUNSHINE.

SOME SHOW UP AS TENDER GREEN LEAVES AND GARDEN PEAS. SUNTAN OIL AND BUGS, MOLASSES IN JANUARY. WEARING FUR COATS AND THERMAL SOCKS. INSECTS IN CASES AND BEARS UNDER ROCKS. RINGS IN TREES AND THE BEHAVIOR OF BEES. IT CROPS UP ALL OVER, AND WE HARVEST THE RESULTS TO MAKE BREAD, BEANS, AND BURGERS.

WHICH GOES TO SHOW THAT WHAT IS A TINY TILT IN THE COSMIC WHEEL, IS A WHOLE WAY OF LIFE FOR SNAKES, SEALS, AND PEOPLE.

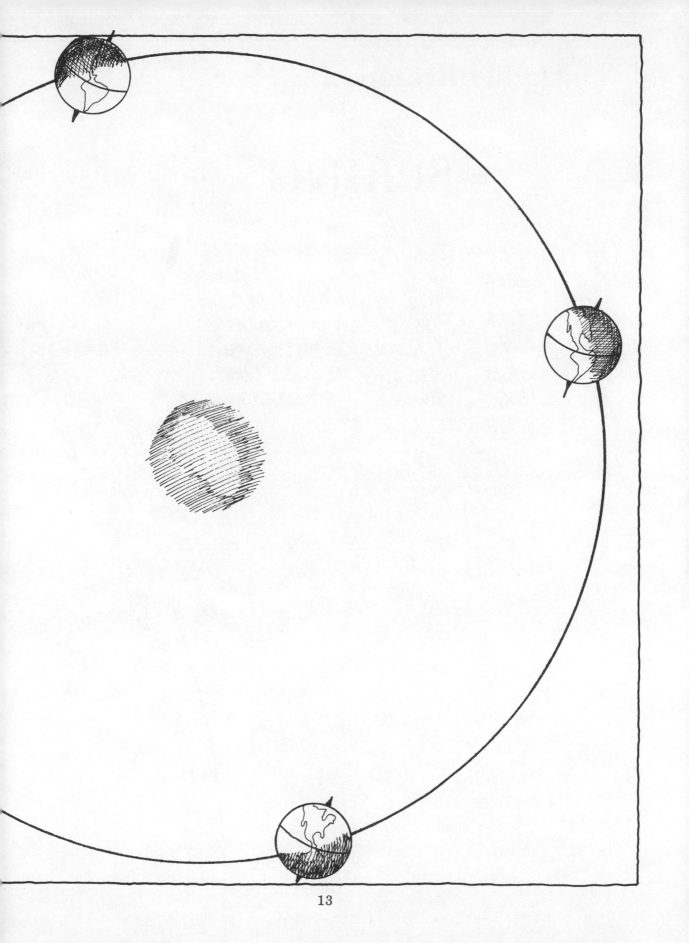

SPRING

SPRING IS WHEN THE HOURS OF LIGHT
BEGIN TO OUTNUMBER THE HOURS OF
NIGHT AND THE EARTH BEGINS TO WARM.
IT'S THE TIME OF THE GREAT AWAKEN-
ING. PLANTS SPRING TO LIFE WITH
NEW GREEN. THE SEVEN SISTERS AP-
PEAR IN THE SKY IN NORTH WEST
BRAZIL, SIGNALING THE TUKANO PEOPLE
THAT IT'S TIME TO PLANT. INSECTS
APPEAR. FISH SPAWN. AMPHIBIANS
LAY THEIR EGGS. IT'S A GOOD TIME
TO BE BORN.

IT LASTS 92 DAYS, 20 HOURS. IT ENDS JUNE 21.

SPRING

SPRING BEGINS MARCH 21.(VERNAL EQUINOX-THE DAY WITH EQUAL DARK.)

SUNDANCE

Star Power

The earth is a star-powered planet. Our star is the sun.

The sun holds the earth in orbit with its great mass. This mass of exploding gas is also the earth's source of light and heat.

Earth's trip around the sun is the reason for winds and rains, summer and winter, and the mysterious cycles of plants and animals.

People used to think that the affairs of the universe were centered around the earth. Now we know that earth affairs are pretty much run by the sun.

Sun

Our sun is a star. It is a mass of hot gasses that explode with energy much the same way a nuclear bomb explodes, only continuously.

The sun has been exploding for 5 billion years at a temperature of over 25,000 degrees Farenheit. It converts about 4 million tons of its mass into heat and light energy every second.

Less than one percent of the sun's energy reaches earth. Even so, that is more than enough energy to meet earth's needs.

Only 1/20 of the sun's energy is used to make the rain fall. Only 1/1,500 is turned into chemical energy by plant life.

In fact, only about three and one-half days worth of the sun's energy is stored on the earth in the form of coal and oil. We are using that total up at a rate of two and a half minutes yearly.

Currently people are working on ways to collect the sun's energy that now goes to waste.

Make a Solar Collector

YOU NEED TWO CANS THE SAME SIZE, BLACK PAINT AND A THERMOMETER. PAINT ONE CAN BLACK. FILL THEM BOTH FULL OF WATER. ON A WARM DAY SET THEM IN THE SUN. AFTER A WHILE TAKE THEIR TEMPERATURES. WHICH ONE COLLECTS THE MOST SOLAR ENERGY? HOW CAN YOU MAKE A BETTER COLLECTOR?

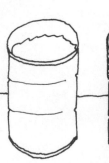

A RADIOMETER WORKS ON THE UNEVEN HEAT COLLECTION PRINCIPLE. HOW CAN YOU PUT THE ENERGY YOU COLLECTED TO WORK?

Sunny Side Up

A LOT OF PEOPLE THINK THAT WE HAVE SUMMER BECAUSE THE EARTH IS CLOSER TO THE SUN. IT IS TRUE THAT THE EARTH DOES ORBIT CLOSER TO THE SUN, BUT THIS HAPPENS DURING THE NORTHERN WINTER.

THE REAL REASON IS THAT BECAUSE THE EARTH TILTS ON ITS AXIS, ONE PART OF OUR WORLD GETS MORE CONCENTRATED SUNLIGHT. ENOUGH TO MAKE THE DIFFERENCE BETWEEN SUMMER AND WINTER. YOU CAN PROVE IT WITH A TIN CAN.

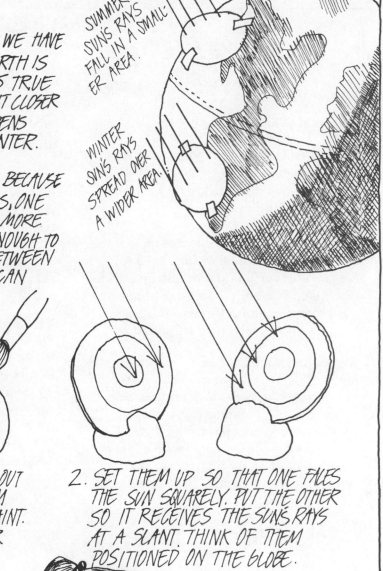

SUMMER SUN'S RAYS FALL IN A SMALLER AREA.

WINTER SUN'S RAYS SPREAD OVER A WIDER AREA.

1. CUT THE TOP AND BOTTOM OUT OF A TIN CAN. PAINT THEM DULL BLACK WITH POSTER PAINT. ROLL SOME CLAY BALLS FOR STANDS.

2. SET THEM UP SO THAT ONE FACES THE SUN SQUARELY. PUT THE OTHER SO IT RECEIVES THE SUN'S RAYS AT A SLANT. THINK OF THEM POSITIONED ON THE GLOBE.

3. AFTER ABOUT TEN MINUTES, TEST THEM ON THE INSIDE OF YOUR ARM. WHICH ONE IS SUMMER?

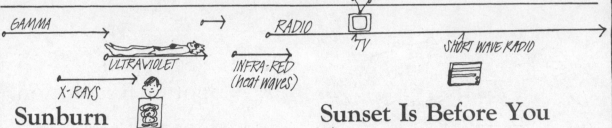

THE SUN'S RAYS RANGE FROM THE SIZE OF ATOMS TO MANY MILES LONG.

GAMMA

ULTRAVIOLET

X-RAYS

RADIO

TV

SHORT WAVE RADIO

INFRA-RED
(heat waves)

Sunburn

The sun radiates a wide spectrum of rays. Some of them we feel as heat, some of them we see as light, and some we detect as x-rays or radio waves.

While our very survival depends on the sun's radiation, not all of the sun's rays are good for earth life. For instance, ultraviolet light is deadly to us earth people and our protoplasm kin. Ultraviolet light can kill cells. Fortunately we are protected.

We live under a thick blanket of atmosphere. The upper atmosphere consists of ozone, which provides a shield from ultraviolet rays. And if some rays get past the ozone layer, we humans have a layer of skin to protect our body. Tanning is our body's way of protecting us from ultraviolet rays.

Heat Trap

The earth's atmosphere also acts as a solar ray collector. Its blanket effect holds heat on earth, preventing the heat from escaping into space. It is this heat that vaporizes water and causes rain.

The sun doesn't shine down in the same amount all over the earth. You noticed with the tin can experiment that the equator gets two and one half times as much heat as the rest of the earth. It is this effect, combined with the earth's spinning, that makes prevailing winds.

Sunset Is Before You Know It

The atmospheric blanket has other talents besides holding heat and screening radiation. It bends light so the sun seems to be a bit higher in the sky than it actually is. You can see this effect after the sun has sunk below the horizon. This bending of light rays also makes the sunset colorful.

Sunlight, after the sun sets, still spills over the horizon. Light rays get bent in different amounts (as in a prism) and separate into bands of color. The bands of color you see above the horizon are arranged in the same order as the color bands in a prism.

What is the final color of a sunset?

YOU CAN SIT UNDER A TABLE AND STILL SEE A LIGHT ON THE TABLE TOP. A BOTTLE OF WATER HAS THE SAME LIGHT BENDING EFFECT AS THE EARTH'S ATMOSPHERE.

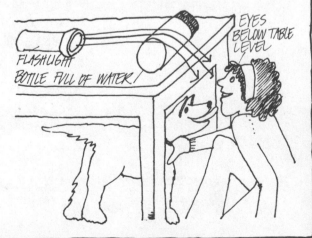

FLASHLIGHT

BOTTLE FULL OF WATER!

EYES BELOW TABLE LEVEL

Spot On

Sunspots were first reported by a Jesuit priest, Father Christoph Scheiner, in 1650. His observations proved to be rather troublesome. Since his church thought of the sun as a symbol of heavenly purity, the thought of spots was not to be tolerated.

Father Scheiner was told that the spots were a figment of his imagination. He was shown conclusively that sunspots did not exist because Aristotle didn't mention them in his astronomy books.

Eleven-Year Spots (or, A Spot of Revolution)

Sunspots have been shown to happen in regular eleven-year cycles. Surprisingly, there are some cycles that seem to show the same eleven-year pattern; water levels in lakes, tree growth rate, atmospheric pressure, and average temperature.

It has been suggested that periods of political unrest and revolution follow the sunspot cycle. The American Revolution, the French revolutions of 1789 and 1848, the Paris Commune, and the Russian revolutions of 1905 and 1917 all occured in years of peak sunspot activity.

See Spots

You can make a pinhole camera to observe the sun easily. With it you should be able to see sunspots.

Sunspots are dark blotches on the sun's face. They are thought to be caused by magnetic storms on the solar surface. They seem to break out periodically and travel across the sun's face in pairs.

Sunspots are of tremendous sizes, some being as large as 50 thousand miles across. Their effects are felt even on earth where the particles they produce block out shortwave radio waves and create the effect of an aurora around the poles.

Try watching sunspots for a period of time. Map their progression across the solar face.

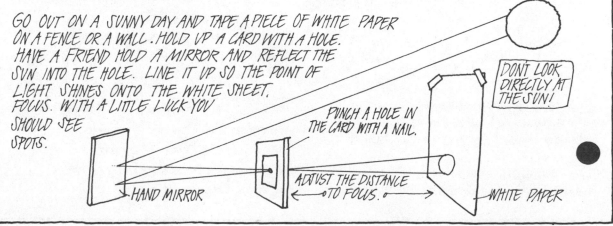

GO OUT ON A SUNNY DAY AND TAPE A PIECE OF WHITE PAPER ON A FENCE OR A WALL. HOLD UP A CARD WITH A HOLE. HAVE A FRIEND HOLD A MIRROR AND REFLECT THE SUN INTO THE HOLE. LINE IT UP SO THE POINT OF LIGHT SHINES ONTO THE WHITE SHEET. FOCUS. WITH A LITTLE LUCK YOU SHOULD SEE SPOTS.

PUNCH A HOLE IN THE CARD WITH A NAIL.

DON'T LOOK DIRECTLY AT THE SUN!

HAND MIRROR

ADJUST THE DISTANCE TO FOCUS.

WHITE PAPER

EOSTER

Easter

The word Easter, according to ancient and Venerable Bede, who was an historian living in England in the eighth century, comes from Eoster. Eoster was the name of the Anglo-Saxon goddess of fertility. Christians celebrate the feast of the resurrection. People nearly everywhere celebrate the return of spring.

The symbols of Easter are much older than Christianity. The egg is everywhere in myth and legend, East and West, as the sign of birth and creation. The hare is an Egyptian symbol of fertility and spring, and it also has lunar associations. So does our Easter.

In the year 325, the date of the Christian celebration was set for the first Sunday following the first full moon after vernal equinox. This was so that pilgrims could travel late to reach the Easter festivals, by the light of the moon.

You Can't Kill Custom

Holidays have been with us since the beginning of man; as long as people have talked of spirits, they have had holiday spirit.

The origins of our days of celebration often are connected to the earth's changes.

The more ancient and more important holidays fall naturally in the places of change in the earth's cycle around the sun.

We celebrate days of lengthening sun at Easter and days of lengthening night at Christmas. The long days of a summer spent are honored at Thanksgiving, not to mention the observance of Groundhog Day.

Cosmic Egg

Eggs have long been a symbol of birth and rebirth — a natural sign of spring.

The peoples of Polynesia, India, Iran, Indonesia, Greece, Phoenicia, Latvia, Estonia, Finland, and ancient America all had legends concerning the birth of earth from an egg.

An Indian legend says the earth was first a non-being, then an egg. For a year it lay, then split into two parts, one of silver, one of gold.

"That which was of gold is the sky.
What was the outer membrane is the mist.
What were the veins are the rivers.
What was the fiend within is the ocean.
Now what was therefrom is yonder sun."

Egg Art

Egg-decorating has been around for a long time.

The Egyptians, Persians, Greeks, and Romans had egg-coloring customs. In some places, eggs were eaten at spring festivals. In other places they were given as gifts and kept as treasures by people who received them.

Edward I gave colored eggs to members of his court. The Russian czars employed Peter Carl Fabergé, who was probably the world's greatest egg artist. In eastern Europe egg decorating became a folk art. Egg art is still fun. Here are some ways to get started.

To Blow an Egg
A lot of egg artists like to work on empty eggs, especially if they will be eggs to keep.

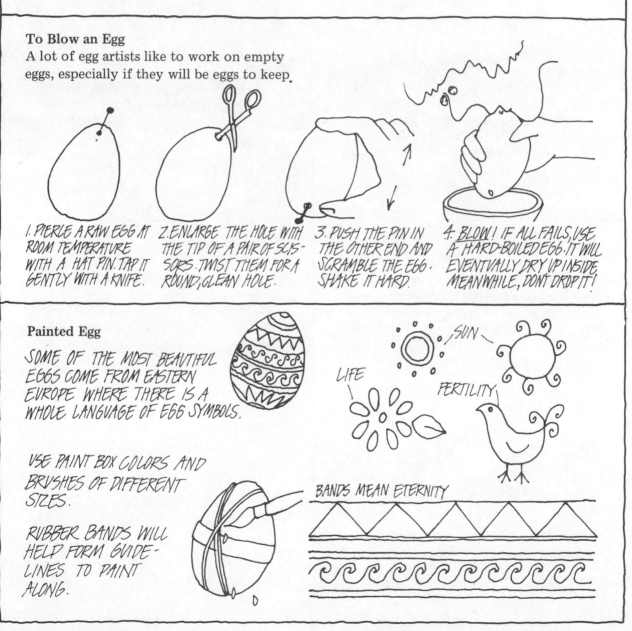

1. PIERCE A RAW EGG AT ROOM TEMPERATURE WITH A HAT PIN. TAP IT GENTLY WITH A KNIFE.

2. ENLARGE THE HOLE WITH THE TIP OF A PAIR OF SCISSORS. TWIST THEM FOR A ROUND, CLEAN HOLE.

3. PUSH THE PIN IN THE OTHER END AND SCRAMBLE THE EGG. SHAKE IT HARD.

4. BLOW! IF ALL FAILS, USE A HARD-BOILED EGG. IT WILL EVENTUALLY DRY UP INSIDE MEANWHILE, DON'T DROP IT!

Painted Egg
SOME OF THE MOST BEAUTIFUL EGGS COME FROM EASTERN EUROPE WHERE THERE IS A WHOLE LANGUAGE OF EGG SYMBOLS.

USE PAINT BOX COLORS AND BRUSHES OF DIFFERENT SIZES.

RUBBER BANDS WILL HELP FORM GUIDELINES TO PAINT ALONG.

SUN

LIFE

FERTILITY

BANDS MEAN ETERNITY

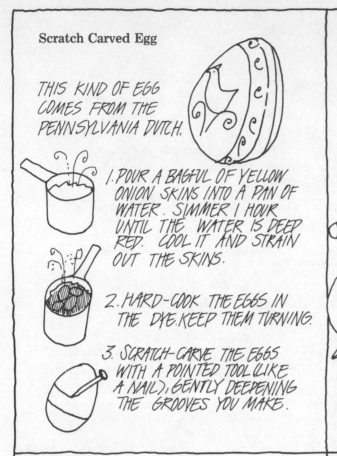

Scratch Carved Egg

THIS KIND OF EGG COMES FROM THE PENNSYLVANIA DUTCH.

1. POUR A BAGFUL OF YELLOW ONION SKINS INTO A PAN OF WATER. SIMMER 1 HOUR UNTIL THE WATER IS DEEP RED. COOL IT AND STRAIN OUT THE SKINS.

2. HARD-COOK THE EGGS IN THE DYE. KEEP THEM TURNING.

3. SCRATCH-CARVE THE EGGS WITH A POINTED TOOL (LIKE A NAIL), GENTLY DEEPENING THE GROOVES YOU MAKE.

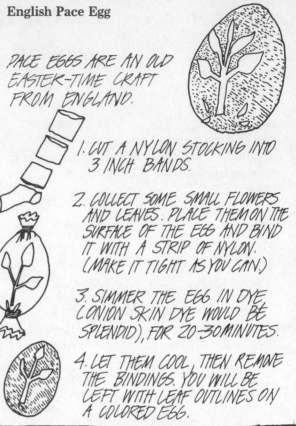

English Pace Egg

PACE EGGS ARE AN OLD EASTER-TIME CRAFT FROM ENGLAND.

1. CUT A NYLON STOCKING INTO 3 INCH BANDS.

2. COLLECT SOME SMALL FLOWERS AND LEAVES. PLACE THEM ON THE SURFACE OF THE EGG AND BIND IT WITH A STRIP OF NYLON. (MAKE IT TIGHT AS YOU CAN.)

3. SIMMER THE EGG IN DYE (ONION SKIN DYE WOULD BE SPLENDID), FOR 20-30 MINUTES.

4. LET THEM COOL, THEN REMOVE THE BINDINGS. YOU WILL BE LEFT WITH LEAF OUTLINES ON A COLORED EGG.

Egg Roll

This is sort of like Destruction Derby. Everyone gets an egg (hard-boiled, please). They can roll it until their egg cracks up. The one who cracks last, wins.

Pace Egging

Find a hill. Everyone starts with an equal number of hard-boiled eggs, colored, of course. Roll 'em. The person who ends up with the most eggs without a crack, wins. Then roll the survivors.

OOLOGY

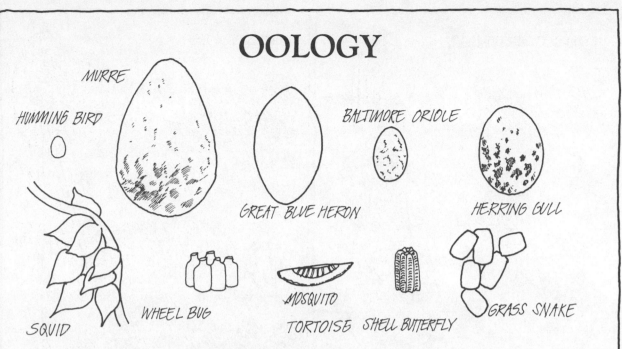

HUMMING BIRD

MURRE

BALTIMORE ORIOLE

GREAT BLUE HERON

HERRING GULL

SQUID

WHEEL BUG

MOSQUITO

TORTOISE SHELL BUTTERFLY

GRASS SNAKE

Oology is the study of eggs. Most animals and plants begin life as an egg cell. A true egg is like a seed. It contains an embryo (undeveloped creature) and materials to keep the embryo alive while it grows inside the protective shell. Some eggs have rigid shells, like chicken eggs. Some have leathery skins and some have thin sacs. Eggs come in a vast number of forms.

Inside Story

Break a hen's egg onto a black surface, so you can look at the parts.

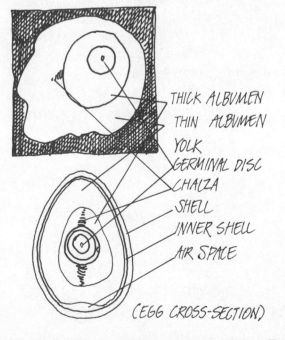

THICK ALBUMEN
THIN ALBUMEN
YOLK
GERMINAL DISC
CHALZA
SHELL
INNER SHELL
AIR SPACE

(EGG CROSS-SECTION)

Shell — mostly calcium, a strong outer coat.

Inner shell — there are actually two. One coats the liquid mass and one coats the inner shell. Each of the coatings allows oxygen to come in.

Air space — the two inner coats separate at the flat end of the shell, to form an air pocket. An older egg has a larger air space caused by evaporation.

Chalza — are stringy things that can twist and hold the yolk in position, sort of like a hammock.

Yolk — is the food supply (there are actually six layers of yellow and six layers of white yolk).

Germinal disc — is the nucleus cell from which a chick would develop if the egg had been fertilized.

Eggs-periment

SOME MORNING WHEN YOU ARE PLANNING TO HAVE SCRAMBLED EGGS, TRY THIS:

STRESS TEST SOME EGGS BY SQUEEZING THEM LENGTHWISE AND CROSSWISE. IT'S SAID NO MATTER HOW STRONG YOU ARE, YOU'LL HAVE A VERY HARD TIME MAKING A BREAK IN ONE DIRECTION. HMMN.....

SOME SCIENTISTS THINK PREHISTORIC BIRDS LAID THEIR EGGS WHILE IN FLIGHT. IMPOSSIBLE YOU SAY?

ONE SCHOOL CLASS DROPPED EIGHTEEN EGGS FROM THE TOP OF A 70 FOOT FIRE LADDER. THREE BROKE. YOU MIGHT TRY AND BREAK THEIR RECORD—IF YOU KNOW A FRIENDLY FIRE FIGHTER.

EVER HAVE THE STICKY SITUATION OF FORGETTING WHICH EGG WAS HARD-BOILED? HERE IS THE SOLUTION:

RAW EGG INSIDE GETS THROWN TO THE OUTSIDE PUSHING IT OUT OF BALANCE

GIVE THE SUSPECTS A GOOD SPIN ON THEIR POINTED ENDS. THE HARD-BOILED ONE WILL ZOOM AROUND WHILE THE RAW ONE WILL TEETER OVER.

KNOW HOW TO TELL A BAD EGG? GIVE IT THE WATER TEST. A BAD EGG WILL FLOAT.

AIR SPACE

EGGS HAVE POROUS SHELLS. AS THEY AGE, THE MOISTURE INSIDE EVAPORATES. THE AIR SPACE INSIDE ENLARGES ENOUGH TO FLOAT THE EGG.

GARBAGE GARDEN

Seeds Want to Grow

Carrot tops are dying to burst out with feathery green foliage.

Potatoes sprout in dark corners when no one is looking.

You probably have the stuff for a rather handsome garden sitting in your garbage can this very moment.

Here are some tricks to turn your garbage into a garden.

Seeds in Soil

You might have heard someone say, "Oh, I'm growing the most wonderful beans." That's not exactly true. Plants grow everywhere — in deserts, in freezing climates, on rocks, in cracks in the streets — without help from anyone.

When you plant something, all you have to do is give it the right environment and wait for it to come alive. Plants need the proper amount of light, water, and air. Also, they need soil. Not just any old dirt from any old where. Resign yourself to heading for the local plant shop (dime store) and buy a bagful of earth.

When you get the soil home, you'll notice that it is light and dark with bits of this and that in it. It's made for plants to be happy in. It has nutrients. It's made to retain water and allows air around plant roots.

1. SAVE YOUR SEEDS FROM APPLES ORANGES, SQUASHES, ANYTHING WITH SEEDS. SOAK THEM IN WATER OVERNIGHT.

2. PLANT THEM IN A SHALLOW PAN (AN EGG CARTON WILL DO FINE). LINE THE BOTTOM WITH SMALL PEBBLES. PUT IN 1½" OF SOIL. PLANT THE SEEDS ¼" DEEP AND 1" APART.

3. MOISTEN THE SOIL AND COVER THE CARTON WITH A PLASTIC BAG TO KEEP IN THE WATER. PUT IT IN A SUNNY WARM PLACE.

4. IN A WEEK OR SO YOU SHOULD SEE SOME SEEDLINGS. WHEN THEY ARE AN INCH OR SO, MOVE THEM TO LARGER POTS.

Tops

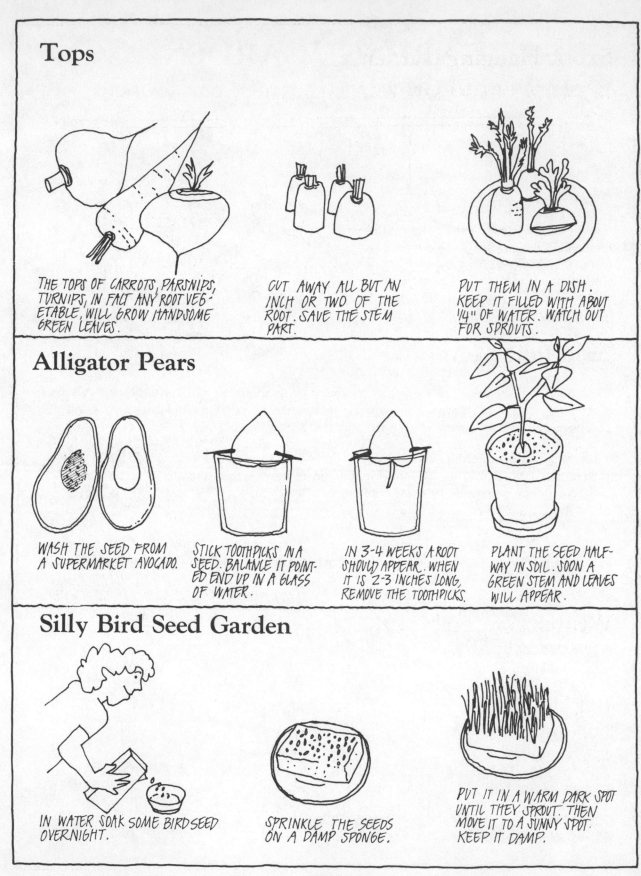

THE TOPS OF CARROTS, PARSNIPS, TURNIPS, IN FACT ANY ROOT VEGETABLE, WILL GROW HANDSOME GREEN LEAVES.

CUT AWAY ALL BUT AN INCH OR TWO OF THE ROOT. SAVE THE STEM PART.

PUT THEM IN A DISH. KEEP IT FILLED WITH ABOUT 1/4" OF WATER. WATCH OUT FOR SPROUTS.

Alligator Pears

WASH THE SEED FROM A SUPERMARKET AVOCADO.

STICK TOOTHPICKS IN A SEED. BALANCE IT POINTED END UP IN A GLASS OF WATER.

IN 3-4 WEEKS A ROOT SHOULD APPEAR. WHEN IT IS 2-3 INCHES LONG, REMOVE THE TOOTHPICKS.

PLANT THE SEED HALFWAY IN SOIL. SOON A GREEN STEM AND LEAVES WILL APPEAR.

Silly Bird Seed Garden

IN WATER SOAK SOME BIRD SEED OVERNIGHT.

SPRINKLE THE SEEDS ON A DAMP SPONGE.

PUT IT IN A WARM DARK SPOT UNTIL THEY SPROUT. THEN MOVE IT TO A SUNNY SPOT. KEEP IT DAMP.

Exotic Hanging Garden

YOU CAN GROW A WINDOW FULL OF TOPSY-TURVY GREENS.

TURN YOUR GARDEN OCCASIONALLY, SO THE FOLIAGE GROWS EVENLY.

USE ANY SORT OF ROOT VEGETABLE LIKE CARROTS, TURNIPS, OR RUTABAGAS. CUT AWAY ABOUT 2/3 OF THE TIP. SCOOP OUT THE CENTER SECTION.

POKE 3 TOOTHPICKS INTO YOUR VEGETABLE. HANG IT WITH A STRING FROM A CURTAIN ROD IN A SUNNY WINDOW. KEEP THE HOLE FILLED WITH WATER.

Winter Garden

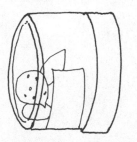

SOME SEEDS ARE DIFFICULT TO SPROUT. SOMETIMES ALL THEY NEED IS AN ARTIFICIAL WINTER IN YOUR FRIDGE.

PUT PEACH, APPLE OR PLUM SEEDS IN A JAR. PUT IT IN YOUR FRIDGE FOR ABOUT 6 WEEKS. TURN THE JAR OCCASIONALLY.

WHEN THEY SPROUT, PLANT THEM IN SOIL. PUT THEM IN A SUNNY WINDOW.

EPIC SPUDS

Tales of a Traveling Tuber

(or, How Do You Like Them Potatoes?)

Despite its rather homely appearance, the potato is very well-traveled and very cultivated.

The potato had been eaten in the Andes region of South America for hundreds of years when Pizarro, a Spanish conquistador, discovered it and took it home to Spain.

The Spanish then took it to Florida.

The British raided the Spanish colonies in Florida and took the tuber to England. There they fed it to pigs.

Louis XVI tried to convince the French people that potatoes were good food and he ordered them served at the palace. Being a real spud booster, he wore potato blossoms in his lapel. But Louis was unsuccessful at popularizing the potato. The French wouldn't eat what the British fed their pigs.

Meanwhile potatoes were exported to Ireland. The Irish, being either smarter or hungrier than other Europeans, took a great liking to potatoes and these tubers became a large part of their diet.

Back in the New World the potato was being grown in Jamestown as cattle food. The English colonists were still convinced that potatoes caused disease. (In fact, potatoes are related to deadly nightshade, and the green parts of the potato plant *are* toxic — but not the tuber.)

Colonists in the New World didn't eat potatoes until 1719 when the Irish came to Londonderry, New Hampshire.

So What's a Tuber?

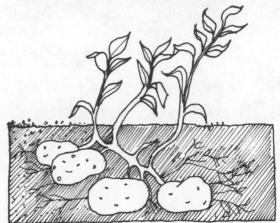

A potato plant has underground stems and roots. The tips of the stems, the tubers, become swollen food storage centers. Tubers are the part you eat.

The "eyes" of a potato are stem and leaf buds. Each chunk of potato with an eye has enough stored food to nourish the buds until green leaves grow and take over the food production.

WHAT HAS EYES BUT CANNOT SEE?

MISSISSIPPI?

A Sprout in the Dark

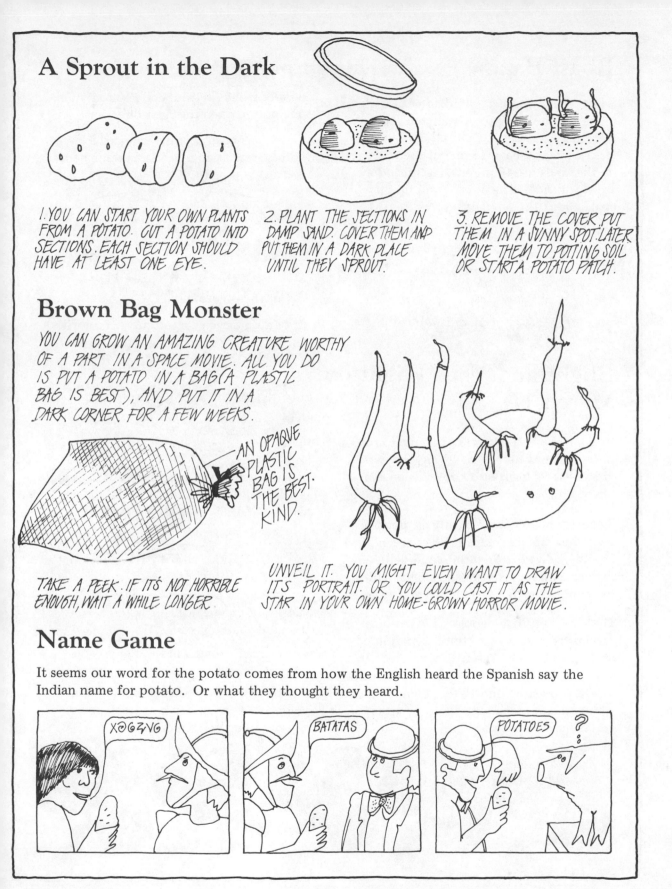

1. YOU CAN START YOUR OWN PLANTS FROM A POTATO. CUT A POTATO INTO SECTIONS. EACH SECTION SHOULD HAVE AT LEAST ONE EYE.

2. PLANT THE SECTIONS IN DAMP SAND. COVER THEM AND PUT THEM IN A DARK PLACE UNTIL THEY SPROUT.

3. REMOVE THE COVER. PUT THEM IN A SUNNY SPOT. LATER MOVE THEM TO POTTING SOIL OR START A POTATO PATCH.

Brown Bag Monster

YOU CAN GROW AN AMAZING CREATURE WORTHY OF A PART IN A SPACE MOVIE. ALL YOU DO IS PUT A POTATO IN A BAG (A PLASTIC BAG IS BEST), AND PUT IT IN A DARK CORNER FOR A FEW WEEKS.

AN OPAQUE PLASTIC BAG IS THE BEST KIND.

TAKE A PEEK. IF IT'S NOT HORRIBLE ENOUGH, WAIT A WHILE LONGER.

UNVEIL IT. YOU MIGHT EVEN WANT TO DRAW ITS PORTRAIT. OR YOU COULD CAST IT AS THE STAR IN YOUR OWN HOME-GROWN HORROR MOVIE.

Name Game

It seems our word for the potato comes from how the English heard the Spanish say the Indian name for potato. Or what they thought they heard.

Roast Batatas

Sometime try eating an Indian potato. It is the simplest way to prepare the food.

Next time you have a fire, put the potatoes on the coals for 40 minutes, or until they are soft inside. The outside will be charcoal. Break them open and feast on the insides.

Blight and Your Plight on March 17

In 1845, 1846, and 1847 the potato crop in Ireland was destroyed by *Phytophtera infestans*, a fungus also known as potato blight.

The Irish people lived mostly on potatoes and when the crop failed they were in great trouble. Five hundred thousand people died as a direct result of the blight. Millions more lost farms and their possessions.

Three million Irish people came to America and brought with them the celebration of St. Patrick's Day. The Irish wear green in honor of St. Pat and they pinch those who forget. So watch out! Wear green on March 17. You can thank your lucky fungus if you forget.

Potato Print

Besides being supertubers, potatoes make fine prints, given the right direction.

To make a potato print you need a large potato, some paper, a felt marking pen, and a stamp pad.

1. Cut the potato in half.

2. Draw a design on the cut surface with a felt marker. Simple designs print best.

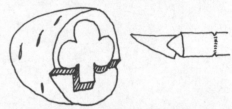

3. Cut away everything but your drawing, using the point of a knife. Make the cut about half an inch deep. Be careful!

4. Press the design onto a stamp pad or on poster paint. Press onto the paper.

Potato prints are good for making do-it-yourself gift wrap paper or book covers — any old thing you think of.

ANIMAL BIRTHDAY

You probably have quite a few animal friends — or at least some passing acquaintances.

Unlike your homo (human) friends, there is a good chance that your animals' birthdays come during one particular part of the year.

Coming up is an animal birthday card that will let you know what some of your animal friends are up to. Also it will tell you what time is the best time to look for a baby turtle and what makes a cat caterwaul.

Sexual Seasons

Since before the earth was inhabited there have been seasons.

Tiny one-celled animals who inhabited the first seas were taking an annual earth trip round the sun. Dinosaurs saw seasons. So did the tiny three-toed horses.

Life on earth grew to expect seasons and adapted ways to live with them. Such seasonal regularity has produced plants and animals with internal timers that signal many patterns in animal behavior. Many animals reproduce on a seasonal timetable.

Spring Is a Fine Time to Be Born

Many animals, especially those native to the far northern or southern latitudes, are born in spring. In spring there is more daylight and increased plant and insect life to provide food for many creatures. In this season there is warmth and the promise of a long easy summer in which to develop before the difficult winter sets in.

For some animals any time is a good time to be born. This is more true for creatures of temperate climates. Humans fall in the *any time* category. So do animals that live in close association with humans, such as flies and mice, who enjoy the comforts of the eternal indoor "spring."

---

gestation - the period after mating and before birth when animal young are forming (embryo stage). This can happen either inside the mother, as with puppies, or outside, as with pigeons (eggs).

31

Animal Birthday Card

ANIMAL	MATING SEASON	GESTATION PERIOD (IN DAYS)	NUMBER BORN, WHERE	OTHER INFORMATION
RABBITS	BREED ALL YEAR, SOMETIMES NOT IN THE WINTER MONTHS.	31	3-9 THE DOE MAKES A NEST OF STRAW AND LINES IT WITH HER FUR.	YOUNG ARE BORN COMPLETELY NAKED AND BLIND. THEIR EYES OPEN IN 9 DAYS. THEY CAN LEAVE THEIR MOTHER IN 2 MONTHS.
CATS	THEY MAY HAVE 3 LITTERS A YEAR. FEMALES MAKE A HORRIBLE, SCREECHY, NOISE CALLED A CATERWAUL TO ATTRACT MALES.	63-65	4-9 KITTENS ARE USUALLY BORN IN CLOSED SPACES (IN CORNERS, BOXES, UNDER BUILDINGS).	KITTENS ARE BORN DEAF, BLIND, AND HELPLESS. THEIR SENSES BEGIN TO OPERATE IN 10-12 DAYS. PURRING IS THOUGHT TO BE A CALL TO FOOD BY THE MOTHER. (GOOD VIBES FOR DEAF KITTENS.)
TURTLES	MATE AND LAY EGGS IN EARLY SPRING OR SUMMER (DEPENDING ON THE BREED).	THE EGGS ARE LAID AND BURIED. THEY HATCH UNATTENDED IN AUGUST—OCTOBER.	YOUNG TURTLES MAY STAY IN THEIR NEST, WITHOUT FOOD, UNTIL THE FOLLOWING SPRING.	SOMETIMES YOUNG TURTLES FROM A SHOP SEEM SLEEPY. THEY MIGHT TRY TO BURY THEMSELVES. LET THEM. THEY MAY HAVE BEEN DUG UP RECENTLY. THEY WILL COME OUT WHEN THEY ARE READY.
CANARIES	ANYTIME	14 (INCUBATION PERIOD)	4-5 EGGS	BABY CANARIES CAN'T FEED THEMSELVES UNTIL THEY ARE 4-5 WEEKS OLD. SINGLE MALE BIRDS MAKE THE BEST SINGERS.

ANIMAL	MATING SEASON	GESTATION PERIOD (IN DAYS)	NUMBER BORN, WHERE	OTHER INFORMATION
HORSES	ANYTIME	340	1	A FOAL IS USUALLY ON ITS FEET WITHIN 2 HOURS OF BEING BORN. THAT'S AN IMPORTANT TALENT WHEN SURVIVAL DEPENDS ON RUNNING.
DOGS	ANYTIME DINGOS (AUSTRALIAN WILD DOGS) MATE ONLY IN FALL. ALL FEMALES IN HEAT SECRETE A SMELL THAT ATTRACTS MALES FOR MILES.	49	SMALL DOGS HAVE 1-2. LARGE DOGS MAY HAVE 10-12	PUPS ARE BORN BLIND AND DEAF. THEIR SENSES BEGIN TO OPERATE IN 14 DAYS. THE BEST AGE TO ADOPT A DOG IS 6-8 WEEKS. A PUP LEFT ON ITS OWN WILL BE WILD BY 14 WEEKS.
SHEEP	USUALLY IN THE FALL	148	1	LAMBS ARE USUALLY BORN IN THE SPRING. IN COLD CLIMATES EARLY LAMBS HAVE A MUCH HARDER TIME SURVIVING.
PIGEONS	PIGEONS ARE MONOGAMOUS (THEY HAVE ONE MATE FOR LIFE.)	14-19 (INCUBATION PERIOD)	2	YOUNG PIGEONS ARE FED "PIGEON MILK," A CHEESY SUBSTANCE FROM STOMACH OF THE ADULT.

FRUIT OR VEGETABLE?

Everyone Knows

Everyone knows that fruit is dessert food. Vegetables are what you have to eat to get dessert. Fruits are sweet. Vegetables aren't.

Right? Wrong.

A botanist, a plant expert, can explain about fruits and vegetables. "The truth is that any plant is a part of the vegetable world, and a fruit is a special part of a seed-producing plant."

After a plant is pollinated the flower turns from an *attractor* to a *protector*. The seeds grow within the walls of the flower. In some plants these walls become thick, fleshy, juicy fruit. Good enough to eat! When you eat the fruit you become an un-suspecting seed mover.

Take a good look at the seeds of some fleshy fruits. They have particularly tough outer jackets. That's so they can pass through the gut of the eater unharmed, to grow wherever they might be deposited.

Give a quiz. Ask anyone which of these are fruits and which are vegetables:

Cucumbers, cherries, berries.
Grapes, melons, peas, bananas, squash.
Tomatoes.

Well?

They are all fleshy fruits, with seeds inside.

Tomato Supreme
(Another "the truth is stranger" story)

In 1820 Robert Gibbon Johnson did a death-defying stunt on the steps of the courthouse in Salem, New Jersey. He ate a tomato.

Some of the assembled crowd were most likely disappointed. They expected him to die promptly. Everyone knew tomatoes were a deadly poison.

In fact, for hundreds of years Europeans had not been eating tomatoes because they all thought the fruit was poisonous. The French grew them as a curiosity and called them *love apples*, fruits to be admired and fondled, but not eaten. Another name for the tomato was *wolf peach* — beautiful but dangerous.

You could call this attitude toward tomatoes silly. You could also call it prejudiced. People who weren't prejudiced against toma-toes were the Indians of Peru and Ecuador. They had been eating tomatoes for thou-sands of years.

From them the practice of eating tomatoes traveled to Europe. Now each American eats about sixty-five pounds of tomatoes every year.

1893 — tomato growers had the United States Supreme Court officially declare the tomato a vegetable (despite its fruit class) in hopes of changing folks' attitude toward tomatoes. Ever have a tomato in a fruit salad?

A Bush Full of Wolf Peaches
(or, How D'ya Like Them Love Apples?)

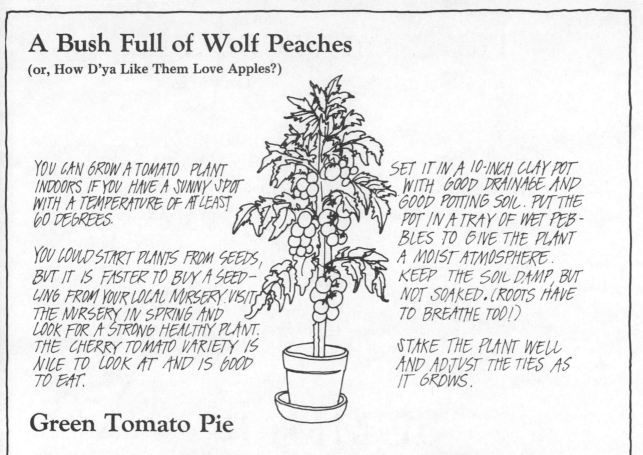

YOU CAN GROW A TOMATO PLANT INDOORS IF YOU HAVE A SUNNY SPOT WITH A TEMPERATURE OF AT LEAST 60 DEGREES.

YOU COULD START PLANTS FROM SEEDS, BUT IT IS FASTER TO BUY A SEEDLING FROM YOUR LOCAL NURSERY. VISIT THE NURSERY IN SPRING AND LOOK FOR A STRONG HEALTHY PLANT. THE CHERRY TOMATO VARIETY IS NICE TO LOOK AT AND IS GOOD TO EAT.

SET IT IN A 10-INCH CLAY POT WITH GOOD DRAINAGE AND GOOD POTTING SOIL. PUT THE POT IN A TRAY OF WET PEBBLES TO GIVE THE PLANT A MOIST ATMOSPHERE. KEEP THE SOIL DAMP, BUT NOT SOAKED. (ROOTS HAVE TO BREATHE TOO!)

STAKE THE PLANT WELL AND ADJUST THE TIES AS IT GROWS.

Green Tomato Pie

Green tomato pie is something to bake when you are feeling adventuresome. This kind of pie doesn't seem so strange when you know that botanists think of tomatoes as large, soft berries. It tastes a little like rhubarb pie.

Finding green tomatoes might be a problem. Ask the grocer if there are any ripening in the back room of the store. Or ask a friend with a garden for some, or gather some from your own bush.

YOU WILL NEED:

5-6 LARGE GREEN TOMATOES   2 TABLESPOONS FLOUR   2 TEASPOONS CINNAMON
3/4 CUP BROWN SUGAR   2 TABLESPOONS VINEGAR   1 PIE CRUST o BUTTER

MY OH MY, GREEN T. PIE!

1. YOU CAN ASK FOR HELP MAKING A CRUST, OR BUY ONE IN THE FROZEN FOODS SECTION AT THE MARKET.
2. CUT THE TOMATOES INTO THIN SLICES. SPRINKLE SALT ON THEM AND LET THEM SIT FOR 30 MINUTES IN A BOWL.
3. SPRINKLE THE FLOUR AND HALF THE SUGAR INTO THE CRUST.
4. PUT IN THE TOMATO SLICES.
5. ADD THE REMAINING SUGAR, CINNAMON AND DOT WITH BUTTER.
6. SPRINKLE ON THE VINEGAR
7. BAKE IN A 375° OVEN FOR ABOUT 40 MINUTES.

SUMMER

AT LAST THOSE SHORTENED NIGHTS AND EXTRA HOURS OF LIGHT BEGIN TO BE FELT. TEMPERATURES RISE. IT'S TIME TO KICK OFF YOUR SHOES AND THINK ABOUT VACATION. IT'S ICE - CREAM WEATHER AND THE 4TH OF JULY, THE DATE THAT MARKS THE APHELION — THE QUIRK IN THE EARTH'S TRIP THAT GIVES THE NORTHERN HEMISPHERE FOUR EXTRA DAYS OF SUMMER. BLOSSOMS TURN TO FRUIT. THE HARVEST BEGINS.

SUMMER SURPLUS

Feast or Famine

There is a basic problem in the world. The food supply is excellent during the summer and rather poor in winter.

Some life forms solve this problem by sleeping through winter (hibernation).

Some move to a sunnier neighborhood (migration).

Some wait out the winter. Human beings are in the group of waiters.

Part of the art of staying alive is knowing how to make summer's food last all year.

This is no easy task since competition for a meal is very stiff among the living.

People have always had to fight insects, rodents, worms, molds, mildews, and various bacteria. They have learned to keep seeds and tubers from consuming themselves in storage.

Throughout the ages people have been developing a whole arsenal of food preservation techniques. You could say they have been explosively successful. (Now their success rests on reserving their numbers so there will be food left to preserve.)

Fruit Leather

ALL YEAR LONG YOU'VE BEEN WAITING AROUND FOR FRESH APRICOTS. THEN SUDDENLY THEY ARE EVERYWHERE, NOT TO MENTION PEACHES AND NECTARINES. NOW WHAT YOU WANT IS PUMPKIN PIE. WELL, HERE IS A WAY TO USE UP EXTRA RIPE FRUIT, AND A WAY TO HAVE SOME APRICOTS WHEN PUMPKIN PIE LOSES ITS CHARM. LOOK FOR FRUIT BARGAINS IN THE OVER RIPE SECTION AT THE MARKET.

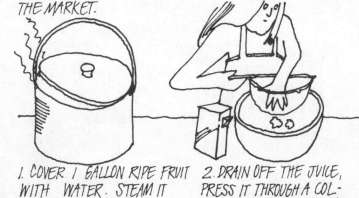

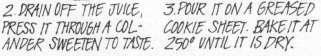

1. COVER 1 GALLON RIPE FRUIT WITH WATER. STEAM IT UNTIL IT IS SOFT.

2. DRAIN OFF THE JUICE, PRESS IT THROUGH A COLANDER SWEETEN TO TASTE.

3. POUR IT ON A GREASED COOKIE SHEET. BAKE IT AT 250° UNTIL IT IS DRY.

4. CUT IT INTO STRIPS.

Fight, Win, Feast

There are many ways to preserve foods but they all do basically the same thing. They make life difficult for the competition by making the food inaccessible (canning), indigestible (pickling), or inhospitable (freezing). The point is to keep foodstuff in a state your competition can't tolerate.

Food for Keeps

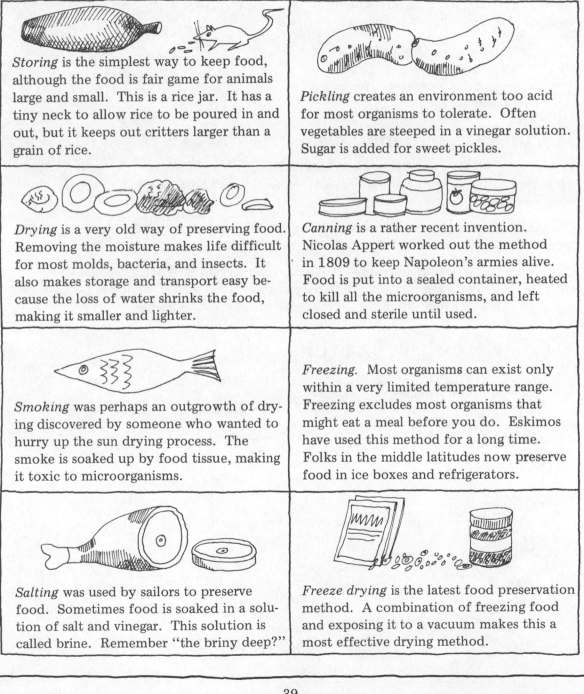

Storing is the simplest way to keep food, although the food is fair game for animals large and small. This is a rice jar. It has a tiny neck to allow rice to be poured in and out, but it keeps out critters larger than a grain of rice.

Pickling creates an environment too acid for most organisms to tolerate. Often vegetables are steeped in a vinegar solution. Sugar is added for sweet pickles.

Drying is a very old way of preserving food. Removing the moisture makes life difficult for most molds, bacteria, and insects. It also makes storage and transport easy because the loss of water shrinks the food, making it smaller and lighter.

Canning is a rather recent invention. Nicolas Appert worked out the method in 1809 to keep Napoleon's armies alive. Food is put into a sealed container, heated to kill all the microorganisms, and left closed and sterile until used.

Smoking was perhaps an outgrowth of drying discovered by someone who wanted to hurry up the sun drying process. The smoke is soaked up by food tissue, making it toxic to microorganisms.

Freezing. Most organisms can exist only within a very limited temperature range. Freezing excludes most organisms that might eat a meal before you do. Eskimos have used this method for a long time. Folks in the middle latitudes now preserve food in ice boxes and refrigerators.

Salting was used by sailors to preserve food. Sometimes food is soaked in a solution of salt and vinegar. This solution is called brine. Remember "the briny deep?"

Freeze drying is the latest food preservation method. A combination of freezing food and exposing it to a vacuum makes this a most effective drying method.

39

Yipes, It's Ripe

A fruit starts out small, hard, and sour. When ripe for the picking it is larger, softer, and sweeter. Just what's happened in between?

At work inside the fruit are substances called *enzymes.* They cause the chemical changes that bring the fruit through the stages of green, rotten, and in-between.

A fruit gets soft because the walls of the cells inside are broken down. It gets sweet because the enzymes turn acids (the sour taste) into sugar.

Fruit looses its green color because the chlorophyll (the substance in plants that turns light into food) collapses. And, most amazing, the fruit begins to emit a special smell, and a most surprising gas.

Mysterious Banana Gas

Farmers in California knew they could harvest all their lemons at once, ripe or not. The lemons could be stored in a room with a kerosene stove and they would all be yellow in a short while.

One grower decided he would warm his lemons with electric heat. To his surprise his crop remained stubbornly green.

In 1924 Dr. Frank Denny discovered that while ripening, fruits exude a peculiar gas called *ethylene,* which is in kerosene smoke. Now many fruits are picked green and gassed with ethylene. This way they are ready to eat at market time, but not before.

A Gas Chamber for Fruits

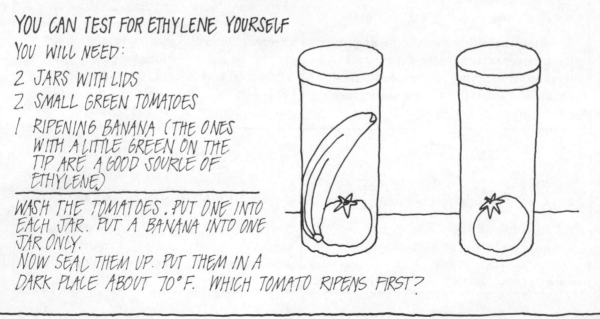

YOU CAN TEST FOR ETHYLENE YOURSELF

YOU WILL NEED:

2 JARS WITH LIDS

2 SMALL GREEN TOMATOES

1 RIPENING BANANA (THE ONES WITH A LITTLE GREEN ON THE TIP ARE A GOOD SOURCE OF ETHYLENE)

WASH THE TOMATOES. PUT ONE INTO EACH JAR. PUT A BANANA INTO ONE JAR ONLY.
NOW SEAL THEM UP. PUT THEM IN A DARK PLACE ABOUT 70°F. WHICH TOMATO RIPENS FIRST?

THE SKY IS FALLING

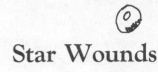

Shooting Stars

Shooting stars or meteors are bits of dust on fire. Space is filled with particles. There are two theories about their origin. One is that they are particles left over after the birth of a planet. The other is that they are debris from a dead planet.

Whatever they are, these particles occasionally collide with the earth. Most of them are tiny, about the size of a grain of sand. They burn up when they enter the earth's upper atmosphere. Their glow is what we call a shooting star.

Falling Star

The Romans believed that every person had a star in the heavens. When you died your star fell from the sky and disappeared.

The following observation was made by Virgil in 40 B.C. According to the date in which this poem was written, he was probably watching a Lyrids shower. Falling stars don't seem to have changed much.

"Often again, a threat of winds you see,
    stars quickly slide across the sky,
Trailing at length upon the black of night,
    white tails of fire."

Star Wounds

A meteorite is a meteor which touches the earth. This happens rarely. Even if a meteor does reach the earth's surface, there is only about one chance in four that it will strike land.

An average of fifteen hundred boulder-sized meteorites crash into earth yearly. Every ten thousand years there is a good chance the earth will be struck by something more the size of a mountain.

Canyon Diablo

A giant meteorite struck the Arizona desert in prehistoric times. It made a crater 600 feet deep and 4,100 feet wide.

Chubb Crater

Quebec, Canada has a crater about twenty miles wide that geologists say is undoubtedly an impact feature.

Siberia

On June 30, 1908 something caused an explosion that was heard for 600 miles around. People more than 100 miles away were knocked over by the shock wave. Trees within a 60-mile radius were flattened. For weeks afterward strange red sunsets were reported from as far away as London. No crater was ever found. Soviet scientists in 1960 theorized the cause of the explosion was a collision of comets.

The Sky Is Falling

(or, The Henny Penny Theory)

On any clear night you can see shooting stars. Some nights you will see more than others. This is because the earth is traveling through an asteroid belt, a band of particles forced by gravity into an orbit around the sun.

Every thirty-three years the earth passes through a dense knot of debris and we see a really spectacular star shower. The year 902 A.D. was the first recorded *year of the stars*. The last was 1965.

Below is a timetable to tell you when the earth will be passing through a swarm of meteors. August is a good month for star showers. The best time to look is after midnight. So, check the chart, pull up a chair, and count your lucky stars.

NAME OF THE SHOWER	NUMBER OF DAYS LONG	DAY OF PEAK ACTIVITY	HOURS OF MAXIMUM ACTIVITY	METEORS PER HOUR (ESTIMATE)
QUADRANTIDS	4	JAN. 3	12-4 A.M.	28
LYRIDS	4	APRIL 22	"	7
ETA AQUARIDS	8	MAY 5	"	7
PONS – WINNECKE	?	JUNE 29	"	?
DELTA-AQUARIS	3	JULY 29	"	27
PERSIDS	25	AUG. 12	"	69
ORACONIDS	1	OCT. 10	"	10
OIONIDS	14	OCT. 20	"	21
LEONIDS	7	NOV. 17	"	21
ANDROMEDES	2	NOV. 21	"	10
GEMINIDS	14	DEC. 13	"	23

Star Dust

The earth collides with millions of meteors and billions of micrometeorites daily. Since the earth's birth this crash course has added about 4 million tons of matter to the earth each year. That is a skin of star dust 10 feet thick.

Meteorites are made mostly of iron and nickel. Both of these elements are magnetic substances. If you drag a magnet over the ground it will pick up some particles. About twenty percent of them will be dust from outer space.

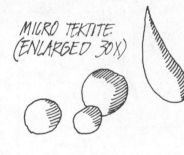

MICRO TEKTITE
(ENLARGED 30X)

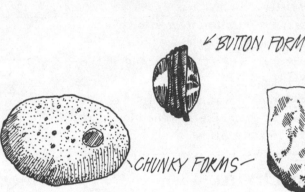

← BUTTON FORM

CHUNKY FORMS →

Tektites

Tektites are terrestrial objects of unknown celestial origin.

They are strange-shaped glassy objects, found only in particular areas of the earth. Scientists know they come from outer space, but they are not sure from where. One theory supposes they are from the earth-moon system.

Tektites have various forms. Some are microsized, some are splash-formed, some are chunky, and some are button-shaped. Scientists are not the only ones fascinated by tektites. The Bushmen of Australia collect them, sometimes carve designs in them, and carry them as charms.

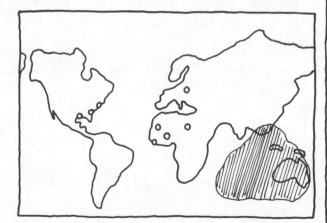

TEKTITES OR MOLDARITES HAVE BEEN FOUND ONLY IN A FEW AREAS OF THE EARTH. MOST COME FROM INDONESIA, AUSTRALIA, AND CZECHOSLOVAKIA.

I AM A YAM
(Or am I?)

I Am a Yam

Yams and sweet potatoes are not the same. Sweet potatoes are the tuberous roots we see being sold in markets and sprouting leaves on window sills. Sweet potatoes have a smooth, red skin and yellow insides. Yams are common in West Africa but seen rarely in America. They have crinkly brown skins and are white or yellow inside.

We can trace almost every plant back to its wild sisters and brothers. The sweet potato has never been found growing wild. It needs a warm climate and pampering because it bruises and rots easily. It is very sensitive.

The sweet potato was first grown in South America. The yam, on the other hand, was found in Asia and Africa.

Mysterious Origins

The first white men to arrive in New Zealand found the natives growing sweet potatoes. The visitors were surprised to hear the potatoes referred to by the same name used by South American Indians. Six thousand miles is a long way for a name to travel.

Vine Divine 1

1. GO TO THE GROCERY STORE AND ASK FOR AN _UNTREATED_ SWEET POTATO. SOMETIMES THEY ARE TREATED TO KEEP THEM FROM SPROUTING.

2. PUT IT IN A GLASS OF WATER. TOOTHPICKS WILL HELP TO BALANCE IT. IT WILL GROW ROOTS, THEN LEAVES IN A FEW WEEKS. CHANGE THE WATER OFTEN.

3. AFTER IT GETS SOME LEAVES, PLANT IT IN A POT WITH SOME SOIL. IT MIGHT GROW TO BE REALLY BIG AND BUSHY.

Vine Divine 2

Vine Divine 3

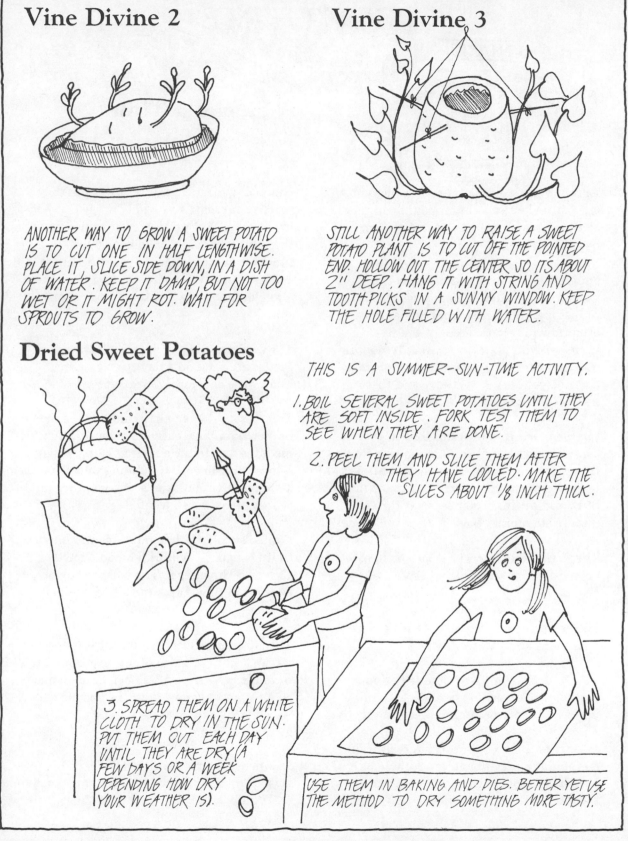

ANOTHER WAY TO GROW A SWEET POTATO IS TO CUT ONE IN HALF LENGTHWISE. PLACE IT, SLICE SIDE DOWN, IN A DISH OF WATER. KEEP IT DAMP, BUT NOT TOO WET OR IT MIGHT ROT. WAIT FOR SPROUTS TO GROW.

STILL ANOTHER WAY TO RAISE A SWEET POTATO PLANT IS TO CUT OFF THE POINTED END. HOLLOW OUT THE CENTER SO ITS ABOUT 2" DEEP. HANG IT WITH STRING AND TOOTH-PICKS IN A SUNNY WINDOW. KEEP THE HOLE FILLED WITH WATER.

Dried Sweet Potatoes

THIS IS A SUMMER-SUN-TIME ACTIVITY.

1. BOIL SEVERAL SWEET POTATOES UNTIL THEY ARE SOFT INSIDE. FORK TEST THEM TO SEE WHEN THEY ARE DONE.

2. PEEL THEM AND SLICE THEM AFTER THEY HAVE COOLED. MAKE THE SLICES ABOUT 1/8 INCH THICK.

3. SPREAD THEM ON A WHITE CLOTH TO DRY IN THE SUN. PUT THEM OUT EACH DAY UNTIL THEY ARE DRY (A FEW DAYS OR A WEEK DEPENDING HOW DRY YOUR WEATHER IS).

USE THEM IN BAKING AND PIES. BETTER YET USE THE METHOD TO DRY SOMETHING MORE TASTY.

ABOUT TIME

NIDERGANG · MITNACHT · AVFGANNG · MITTAG

BERG DES DERDAVM DAVMES LINGEDES LEBES

SEIG FINGER 6 MITELFINGER GOLTFINGR 7 ORFINGER 8 5 4 3 2 1

HAND SUNDIAL
POCKET SUNDIAL

JAN DEC FEB NOV MAR OCT

A Step at a Time

People have been marking time by the sun for many millennia.

An hour can seem like forever when you are at the dentist. But an hour is no time at all when you are having fun with your best friend.

People have been thinking about time and ways to keep track of it throughout most of history. At the dawn of humanity (and even now in remote areas of the world) there were no hours and certainly no minutes or seconds. These measures of time had not yet been invented — and there was no need for them.

Simple-living folk measure time in cycles. They observe sunrise and moon rise, daytime and nighttime. They measure time in cycles of the moon, seasons, growth, and birth and death. Their sense of time is an unhurried, eternal one.

There are other ways to think of time. Historians think of time as a series of events.

Politicians think of time in terms of five-year plans and future elections.

In school kids think of time as periods — math periods, reading periods, and lunch periods, not to mention recess and vacation.

Scientists think of time as intervals. Time to them is a precise and measurable unit of length, whether it is measured in microseconds or in light years.

Gradually, after careful observation, they worked out ways to divide days using shadow devices. But no matter how ingenious they were, people still had to adjust their timekeeping for longer days in the summer and shorter days in winter. And there were also cloudy days when there was no sunshine.

The earliest timekeeping methods were pretty tiresome on a day-to-day basis. They were also rather inaccurate.

The present-day clock has undergone many refinements since early-day devices. Archimedes is said to have used a falling weight to measure time. But a falling weight needs a brake, so various kinds of regulators and gear systems were invented.

Galileo's work with pendulums was applied to timekeeping by a Dutchman named Christian Huyghens. The balance wheel later made time measurable in even smaller intervals.

The alternating electric current was applied to clock knowledge and now even the rate of radioactive decay has been used to make an all-time, super accurate atomic clock which is able to measure the most minute amounts of time.

So when you call the time lady and she says, "The time is four twenty-two, exactly," you'll appreciate how right she is.

Make Time

You can make an assortment of time-keepers. Here are clocks to make that keep track of hours by timing a physical phenomenon. These clocks were all used before the invention of the mechanical clock (which turned out to be a real time saver).

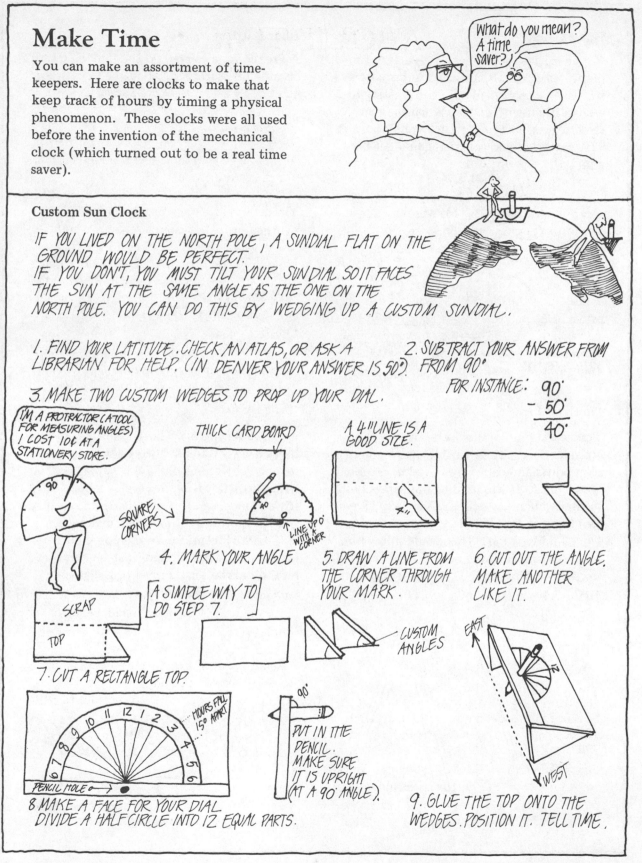

Custom Sun Clock

IF YOU LIVED ON THE NORTH POLE, A SUNDIAL FLAT ON THE GROUND WOULD BE PERFECT.
IF YOU DON'T, YOU MUST TILT YOUR SUNDIAL SO IT FACES THE SUN AT THE SAME ANGLE AS THE ONE ON THE NORTH POLE. YOU CAN DO THIS BY WEDGING UP A CUSTOM SUNDIAL.

1. FIND YOUR LATITUDE. CHECK AN ATLAS, OR ASK A LIBRARIAN FOR HELP. (IN DENVER YOUR ANSWER IS 50°)

2. SUBTRACT YOUR ANSWER FROM FROM 90°

FOR INSTANCE:
```
  90°
- 50°
  40°
```

3. MAKE TWO CUSTOM WEDGES TO PROP UP YOUR DIAL.

I'M A PROTRACTOR (A TOOL FOR MEASURING ANGLES) I COST 10¢ AT A STATIONERY STORE.

THICK CARD BOARD

SQUARE CORNERS

LINE UP 0° WITH A CORNER

A 4" LINE IS A GOOD SIZE.

4. MARK YOUR ANGLE

5. DRAW A LINE FROM THE CORNER THROUGH YOUR MARK.

6. CUT OUT THE ANGLE. MAKE ANOTHER LIKE IT.

CUSTOM ANGLES

SCRAP

TOP

A SIMPLE WAY TO DO STEP 7.

7. CUT A RECTANGLE TOP.

HOURS FALL 15° APART

PENCIL HOLE

8 MAKE A FACE FOR YOUR DIAL DIVIDE A HALF CIRCLE INTO 12 EQUAL PARTS.

90°
PUT IN THE PENCIL. MAKE SURE IT IS UPRIGHT (AT A 90° ANGLE).

EAST

WEST

9. GLUE THE TOP ONTO THE WEDGES. POSITION IT. TELL TIME.

What do you mean? A time saver?

Water Clock

For centuries the Chinese used a very simple water clock. It consisted of a shallow pan with a very small hole in it, resting in a bowl filled with water. When the pan sank, a gong was rung to mark the hour. This sort of clock watching could get boring.

A PLASTIC PLATE WITH A SMALL HOLE

A LARGE PAN FILLED WITH WATER

WHEN THE PLATE SINKS, YOU CAN SOUND THE GONG.

Hour Bottles

A French monk invented the sand clock because his water clock had the irritating habit of freezing up in cold weather.

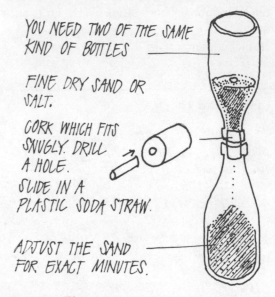

YOU NEED TWO OF THE SAME KIND OF BOTTLES

FINE DRY SAND OR SALT.

CORK WHICH FITS SNUGLY. DRILL A HOLE.
SLIDE IN A PLASTIC SODA STRAW.

ADJUST THE SAND FOR EXACT MINUTES.

Tin Can Clock

This is the kind of clock the Greeks and Romans used. Their version was made of clay bowls and called a *clepsydra*, meaning water thief. It was used to time speeches in the Roman law courts. A sneaky lawyer would bribe the attendant to fill the clock with muddy water. This would allow him to speak longer because his time would *flow* more slowly.

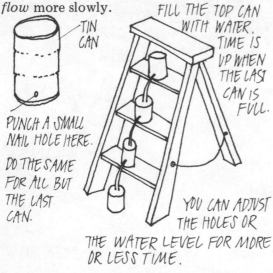

TIN CAN

FILL THE TOP CAN WITH WATER. TIME IS UP WHEN THE LAST CAN IS FULL.

PUNCH A SMALL NAIL HOLE HERE.

DO THE SAME FOR ALL BUT THE LAST CAN.

YOU CAN ADJUST THE HOLES OR THE WATER LEVEL FOR MORE OR LESS TIME.

Time By Fire

Another very exotic alarm clock was sometimes used in China. Two brass balls were suspended from either end of a piece of string, which was placed across a burning stick of incense. In time the string burnt, and the balls fell into a bowl, making a loud enough clank to awaken people. The people could then congratulate each other on their cleverness in inventing such a sweet-smelling alarm clock.

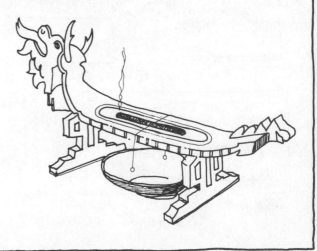

NAVIGATION

A Navigation Story

In 1707 Sir Cloudsley Shovel mistook his longitude and ran into the Scilly Islands, which wasn't as silly as it sounds.

Four ships and 2,000 men were lost, including Sir Cloudsley. The government, after a study of the disaster, in 1714 offered a prize of 20,000 pounds (approximately $875,000 in today's American money) for a method of determining longitude to within one-half of a degree.

Sir Isaac Newton considered the problem and said what was needed was a watch to keep exact time. A tricky problem to have exact time on board a ship that moves in rough seas.

In 1728 John Harrison did some drawings and six years later he came up with seventy-two pounds worth of *chronometer* (an exceptionally precise clock).

HARRISON BUILT FOUR MODELS OF HIS CHRONO-METER. THE LAST WAS A STREAMLINED VERSION ABOUT THE SIZE OF AN ALARM CLOCK. IT WAS SO ACCURATE IT LOST ONLY 15 SECONDS ON A FIVE MONTH TRIP TO JAMAICA. ABOVE IS A NEWER VERSION.

Sometimes Minutes Mean Miles

LATITUDE
LONGITUDE

In order to prevent great catastrophes and loss of life it was necessary to refine the art of navigation.

A sailor could already determine his latitude (his position north or south of the equator) with an *astrolabe* (an instrument used to tell the altitude of the sun). But he needed to know more. He needed to know his longitude, or position along the equator.

The earth has been conveniently divided into twenty-four grapefruit sections, one for each hour of the day. These sections are indicated by the longitude lines on maps. Each of these sections is divided into sixty parts called *minutes*, so that the earth, all sliced and sectioned, reads like a wrist watch.

So if a mariner, as Newton suggested, keeps one clock set at Greenwich time, which is the starting place for longitude numbers, and compares it to his local time, he can compute where he is on the giant clock face, earth.

Navigation Tricks

You might want to do a little navigation on your own. Here are some tricks to try out. You are a first-class navigator if you can explain why these tricks work.

Direction from a Wrist Watch

YOU CAN FIND YOUR DIRECTION WITH A WATCH, IF IT IS SET FOR THE CORRECT TIME, AND IF THE SUN IS CASTING A SHADOW.

(ADD 1 HOUR FOR DAY LIGHT SAVING TIME.)

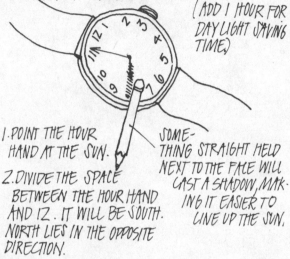

1. POINT THE HOUR HAND AT THE SUN.

2. DIVIDE THE SPACE BETWEEN THE HOUR HAND AND 12. IT WILL BE SOUTH. NORTH LIES IN THE OPPOSITE DIRECTION.

SOMETHING STRAIGHT HELD NEXT TO THE FACE WILL CAST A SHADOW, MAKING IT EASIER TO LINE UP THE SUN.

How Much Light Till Night?

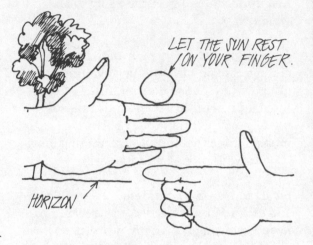

LET THE SUN REST ON YOUR FINGER.

HORIZON

EACH FINGER BETWEEN THE SUN AND THE HORIZON EQUALS 15 MINUTES UNTIL SUNSET. SO FIVE FINGERS MEAN YOU CAN ESTIMATE 1 HOUR AND 15 MINUTES.

Direction from a Shadow Stick

1. PUT A STICK WHERE IT WILL THROW A SHADOW.

2. MARK THE SHADOW TIP AT SUNRISE.

3. WITH A STRING DRAW AN ARC.

4. AT SUNSET MARK WHERE THE SHADOW TOUCHES THE ARC.

5. THE HALFWAY POINT BETWEEN THE MARKS, ALONG THE ARC, WILL BE SOUTH.

Needle Compass

THIS ONE CAN BE DONE WITH A BIT OF CAREFUL HANDLING.

1. RUB THE NEEDLE CAREFULLY IN ONE DIRECTION ONLY WITH A BIT OF SILKY CLOTH. DO IT 100 TIMES.

2. LOWER IT CAREFULLY INTO A CUP OF STILL WATER. THE SURFACE TENSION WILL ALLOW IT TO FLOAT.

3. IF IT IS AWAY FROM METAL OBJECTS, THE THE EYE WILL SWING AROUND POINTING NORTH, IF YOU RUBBED IT POINT TO EYE.

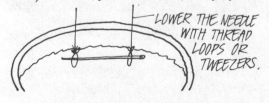

LOWER THE NEEDLE WITH THREAD LOOPS OR TWEEZERS.

BODY CLOCKS

Slumber Party

Have you ever been awake all night? By the next morning you should be very sleepy, right?

Wrong. What normally happens is that you are wide awake. Not to say that you won't miss those hours of sleep later in the day, but now you can't sleep for anything. Your body clock knows it's morning.

Body clocks are interesting mechanisms that people are just beginning to understand. Before animals and plants, before the earth had seas or air, there was day and night and there were seasons.

Almost all organisms evolved with a way of predicting these changes — with an internal clock to time sleeping, waking, migrating, flowering. It's like having the seasons under their skin.

Circadian Rhythms — are daily cycles of organisms which are determined by night patterns.

Circanian Rhythms — are yearly cycles of organisms which are determined by seasonal patterns.

Palolo Is Never Wrong

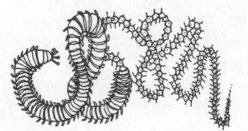

An amazing body clock belongs to a worm, the palolo worm, who lives on the docks of the shores of Fiji and Samoa. On these Pacific shores day length and temperature change only a little.

It is unlikely that you will ever meet a palolo worm, unless you are on the rocky shores of Tahiti or Samoa in October or November on the day the moon enters its last quarter (or the day before) at dawn.

What Time Is Your Body?

Did you know that your heart beats slower between 10 P.M. and 7 A.M.?

That your body temperature falls during sleep?

That your oxygen consumption peaks during your normal period of highest activity — whether you're active or not?

That sodium and potassium excretion in your body is highest at mid-day, and lowest at mid-night, no matter what you eat or when you sleep?

Instead of asking someone what time it is, it might be wiser to ask yourself, "what time's my body?"

I Got Rhythm

It might be interesting to look at your own body clock, to see what your natural pattern of sleeping and waking is like. Try this experiment during vacation, when there aren't too many other things to do. Get permission from your parents before you start. Don't do this if you are sick.

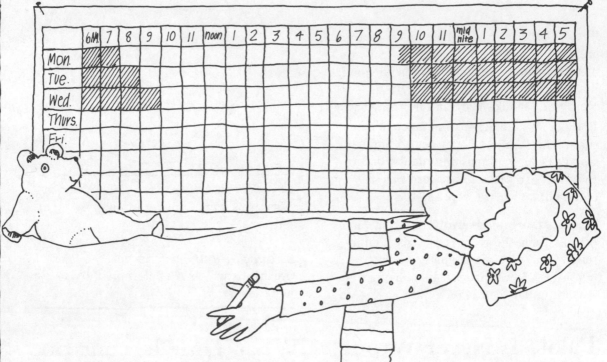

Make a chart like the one above to keep a record of your sleeping and waking hours. Color in the blocks of time in which you are awake.

The object of this activity is not to change your pattern, but to record it. Go to sleep when you are tired, get up when you are awake. Try not to think about the time while you are charting your hours. Keep the record for at least a week (the longer the better). When you finish the chart, look back and check for a pattern.

Body Clocks Are Not Exact

They need a certain amount of resetting. Your body clock seems to take its cues from sunrise and sunset.

Michel Sittre put himself in an environment where there were no clues to let him know what time of day or night it was. He was in a cave 375 feet below ground near the Alps. His day to emerge, September 14, came long before he thought it was due. He had been underground for sixty-two days, although according to his body clock it was only August 20.

Good Time Garden

You could have a time-keeping garden if you had the space, and perhaps some help from your mom and dad. Flower clocks were popular in old formal European gardens.

This one will work in North America and is accurate to the ½ hour on sunny days. You could plant some of the clock or just one plant.

Spotted Cat's Ear O 6 AM	African Marigolds O 7 AM	Mouse ear Hawkweed O 8 AM	Prickly Sow Thistle ⊗ 9 AM	Star of Bethlehem O 11 AM	Passion Flower O 12
Evening Primroses O 6 PM	White Waterlily ⊗ 5 PM	Small Bindweed ⊗ 4 PM	Scarlet Pimpernel ⊗ 2 PM	Childing Pink ⊗ 1 PM	

O = Opening Time →
⊗ = Closing Time

Hours by Flowers

If you can't make a floral clock, you could have a pot of time-telling flowers, even indoors.

You might plant morning glories or Peruvian Marvels. You can get the seeds at most seed stores. Follow directions on the back of the seed pack. Put the pots in a sunny place.

WORM FARM

What Do You Mean, a Worm?

People call anything small that crawls without legs, a *worm*. We give the name "worm" to some snakes and lizards, to some mollusks (which are kinds of spineless animals), and to young insects. That's not right.

A worm is a special sort of creature. It is not a snake because it doesn't have a backbone, and it is not a lizard, because it doesn't have legs, although it does have feet. A worm is not a caterpillar.

There are 20,000 species of worms. They inhabit every region of the world except the polar and high mountain areas. Some burrow or crawl on land, some swim in water, and some attach themselves to rocks and the insides of other animals. A very important worm is the earthworm.

A Flaccid Worm Is a Feeble Worm

The earliest worms were water creatures. Modern earthworms are soft and naked animals that live in moist soil. They leave their burrows only in the cool, damp night and when it rains.

A worm is something like a water bed. It has what is called a *hydrostatic skeleton*, which is a cavity between its muscles and its gut which contains fluid. This fluid gives the body shape and makes the worm a flexible, fluid critter, ideal for making tunnels and burrowing.

Worm Work

Earthworms are an invisible superforce. It is is estimated that in old grassland there are about 3 million worms per acre. In one year they might bring ten tons of soil to the surface. To accomplish this they must do a lot of gnawing and burrowing.

Charles Darwin was a worm watcher. In 1842 he spread chalk and ashes over an area of ground. Thirty years later the layer was buried under seven inches of soil. Darwin concluded that the surface soil had been through the guts of numerous worms, and that large stones and old buildings are slowly sinking below the surface of the earth with all that underground activity.

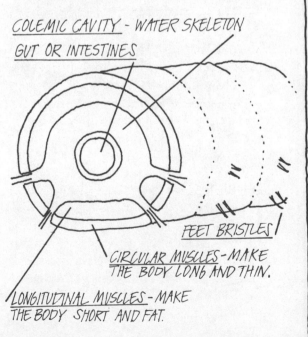

CROSS SECTION OF A WORM
(WORM STEAK)

COLEMIC CAVITY - WATER SKELETON
GUT OR INTESTINES

FEET BRISTLES

CIRCULAR MUSCLES - MAKE THE BODY LONG AND THIN.

LONGITUDINAL MUSCLES - MAKE THE BODY SHORT AND FAT.

Worm Anatomy (Worm Terms)

BRAIN - UNDER SEGMENT 3. IT IS PRIMITIVE, BUT HAS KEPT WORMS ALIVE FOR HUNDREDS OF MILLIONS OF YEARS.

FOOD STORAGE AND GIZZARD - UNDER SEGMENTS 15-19.

INTESTINES - FROM GIZZARD TO THE WORM'S END.

FEET OR SETAE - THERE ARE TWO PAIR ON EVERY SEGMENT. YOU CAN FEEL THEM BY GENTLY RUBBING THE UNDER SIDE OF A WORM.

MOUTH - BETWEEN SEGMENT 1 AND THE KNOB END. YOU CAN SEE IT IF YOU LOOK WITH A HAND LENS.

HEART - BETWEEN SEGMENT 5 AND 11. BELOW IS A CUT-AWAY PICTURE OF THE HEART.

Reproduction — worm cocoons, which store eggs, are made in segments 32 through 37. The slimy (mucous) cocoon holds small eggs. When eggs are ready to hatch, the worm slips the cocoon over its head. Worms hatch out when cocoon plugs dissolve.

No lungs or gills — the worm breathes through its skin.

Hydrostatic skeleton — a worm has no bones.

Count the segments — an adult worm will have 115 to 120 segments. Young worms have less.

Worm Walk

When a worm wants to move forward, its powerful muscles contract and it squeezes itself around the middle (sort of like when you squeeze a tube of toothpaste). The worm's front gets long and thin and burrows ahead. Then another set of muscles squeezes and makes the worm fat. It pushes its feet down and grips the burrow while the rear section catches up with the front section.

Earthworms can force their way through soft earth; they must eat their way through harder soil. Eaten earth passes through their alimentary canal (gut) and is deposited on the ground's surface as _castings_.

DIRECTION OF SQUEEZING (WAVES) o→

DIRECTION OF WORM ←o

How to Catch a Worm

1. Get permission to dig in your back yard. Anywhere there's soil.

2. Check for castings (a casting will look like a crumbly pile of dirt heaped up in one spot on the ground) during the day. Mark them. After sunset return to the spots. Quietly, using no light, look around. The worm will be half in and half out of its burrow. Surprise it before it springs back into its hole.

HINT: SOME WORM HUNTERS TAP THE GROUND OR SOUND AN ALARM CLOCK. THE VIBES HELP SCARE UP WORMS.

How to Handle a Worm

Worms are harmless, soft animals. Be careful! They break if they are squashed or jerked. If you do break one while pulling it from its burrow, keep the broken piece in your worm farm. It might grow into a whole new worm. These animals can grow new parts. This ability is called the power of *regeneration*.

How to Feed a Worm

At night worms drag leaves and decaying matter into their burrows. They eat the vegetable matter in soil as well as leaves.

You might provide your worm farm with a salad of lettuce, carrot scrapings, cabbage, or even bits of hamburger.

How to House a Worm

YOU WILL NEED A BIG JAR (ABOUT QUART SIZE) SOME SOIL, SOME SAND, DARK PAPER, TAPE. THIS SIZE JAR IS A GOOD SIZE FOR TWO WORMS.

FILL THE JAR WITH DAMP SOIL. ALTERNATE WITH A LAYER OF SAND. IN A FEW DAYS THE LAYERS WILL VANISH. WHY IS THAT?

WORMS ARE LIGHT SHY. IF YOU WANT TO SEE THEM BURROWING, WRAP THE JAR WITH DARK PAPER. LOOK AT THEM IN A DIM LIGHT. DON'T FORGET TO FEED THEM.

LID WITH HOLES

SOIL

SAND

SOIL

SAND

YEAST BEAST FEAST

Yeasts

Yeasts have been an important force on earth for a long time. They were some of the original colonizers of the prehistoric seas and added a lot of very important carbon dioxide to the atmosphere.

Since biblical times, and probably before, yeasts have been making bread rise and people sing loud songs in honor of the wine they ferment.

Yeasts are tiny, one-celled plants. They are distant cousins of the mushroom. Like mushrooms, they contain no chlorophyll, so they must turn their surroundings into food. Yeasts convert sugar into alcohol and carbon dioxide. To do this, they require rather sweet surroundings.

Breath of Life

There are many ways to breathe.

Green plants breathe in carbon dioxide and breathe out oxygen. We breathe in oxygen and breathe out carbon dioxide.

Yeasts don't breathe in anything (or almost nothing) and yet they breathe out carbon dioxide. They are a very ancient kind of life. They arose in the primeval seas in the days when earth had little oxygen, so they learned to live without it.

Meanwhile their production of carbon dioxide helped create an atmosphere that allowed for the development of green plants.

Germ Theory

French winemakers of the nineteenth century wondered why sometimes wine turned into an awful, sour liquid instead of the prize wine they wanted. They asked Louis Pasteur, an already famous scientist, to consider the problem.

The winemakers thought the yeast was a chemical agent. Pasteur contended that yeast was a living thing — an unconventional idea to say the very least! Pasteur was crazy! Table wine alive? Impossible!

Eventually Pasteur developed a way of dealing with germs. He heated a liquid, killing the invisible life, then quickly cooled it.

pasteurization - this sterilization process was named after its inventor, Louis Pasteur. A hundred years later you find his name remembered on milk cartons everywhere.

Yeasts Multiply by Dividing

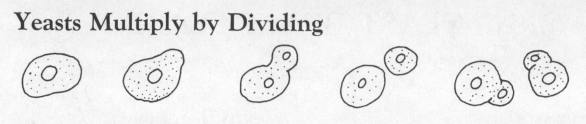

This is a drawing of how a yeast plant forms a bud. It gets larger and finally splits off into a new and entirely separate plant. All this takes about fifteen minutes.

Yeasts can double their number in fifteen minutes. In thirty minutes there are four times as many. In an hour there are sixteen times as many and at the end of two hours there are 256 times as many yeast plants as you had at the beginning of the experiment. (This sort of growth is called *exponential* growth.)

Another way to think of this growth is suppose you have four friends over for milk and cookies. Multiplying at the rate of yeast, in two hours there would be 1,024 people around your kitchen table. Pretty soon you would run out of milk and cookies.

It's the same with yeasts. The vast population soon uses up all the available food, if it doesn't first kill itself in its own wastes (alcohol). Meanwhile all those yeast plants have breathed out a lot of carbon dioxide. So, make all those friends some pretzels if you run out of cookies.

15 MINUTES _____

30 MINUTES _____

45 MINUTES _____

1 HOUR _____

1 HOUR, 15 MINUTES

HEY, STOP PUSHING!

Yeast Breath

If you had a microscope you could see yeast cells bud and divide. But even without a microscope you can watch yeasts breathe.

Try this experiment to see what conditions yeasts like best:

YOU NEED 1 PACKAGE DRY YEAST, A THERMOMETER, SUGAR, AND SALT.

¼ TEASPOON SUGAR

¼ TEASPOON SUGAR + ¼ TEASPOON SALT

DON'T ADD ANYTHING

1   2   3

DISSOLVE THE YEAST IN 1 CUP 85° WATER. POUR EQUAL AMOUNTS OF THE YEAST INTO 3 GLASSES. STIR IN THE SUGAR AND SALT. PUT THE GLASSES INTO A WARM WATER BATH. WHICH YEASTS ARE THE LIVELIEST? NOW TURN THEM INTO PRETZELS.

Pretzels

YOU CAN MAKE PRETZELS USING THE YEAST BREATH EXPERIMENT.

↙ YOU MIGHT ASK FOR SOME ADULT MUSCLE DOING THIS STEP.

1. POUR THE CONTENTS OF ALL THREE GLASSES INTO A BOWL. SLOWLY STIR IN ABOUT 4 CUPS FLOUR.

2. STIR IT UNTIL IT ALL STICKS TOGETHER IN A FAIRLY DRY WAD IN THE BOTTOM OF YOUR BOWL. YOU MIGHT NEED MORE FLOUR.

10 MINUTES?

3. YOU NEED TO KNEAD THE DOUGH TO MAKE IT SMOOTH AND STRETCHY.

FOLD OVER THE DOUGH

THEN PRESS IT DOWN. TURN IT A QUARTER.

AND REPEAT. KNEAD IT FOR 10 MINUTES

COVER IT WITH A CLOTH AND LEAVE IT IN A WARM SPOT.

THERE'S NO RULE ABOUT PRETZEL SHAPES

BAKE FOR 10 MINS. AT 475°

MIX 1 EGG YOLK + 1 T. WATER.

SPRINKLE WITH SALT

4. WHEN IT HAS DOUBLED IN SIZE, ROLL IT OUT ON A FLOURED SURFACE.

5. CUT IT INTO STRIPS AND SHAPE THE DOUGH INTO PRETZELS.

6. PAINT THEM WITH EGG YOLK. PUT THEM ON A BAKING SHEET, LET THEM RISE TO TWICE THEIR SIZE. THEN BAKE.

GINGER BEER IS COMING UP

Ginger Beer

GINGER BEER IS AN OLD-FASHIONED FIZZY DRINK THAT'S EASY TO MAKE. THIS IS A RECIPE FOR TWO QUARTS. IF YOU REALLY LIKE IT, DOUBLE THE AMOUNTS THE NEXT TIME YOU BREW SOME.

1/2 OZ. ROOT GINGER

1 CUP SUGAR

1/2 TABLESPOON CREAM OF TARTAR

1/2 TABLESPOON DRY PACKAGED YEAST

1 LEMON

2 TABLESPOONS SUGAR

1/2 GALLON BOILING WATER

2 QUART BEER BOTTLES WITH TOPS

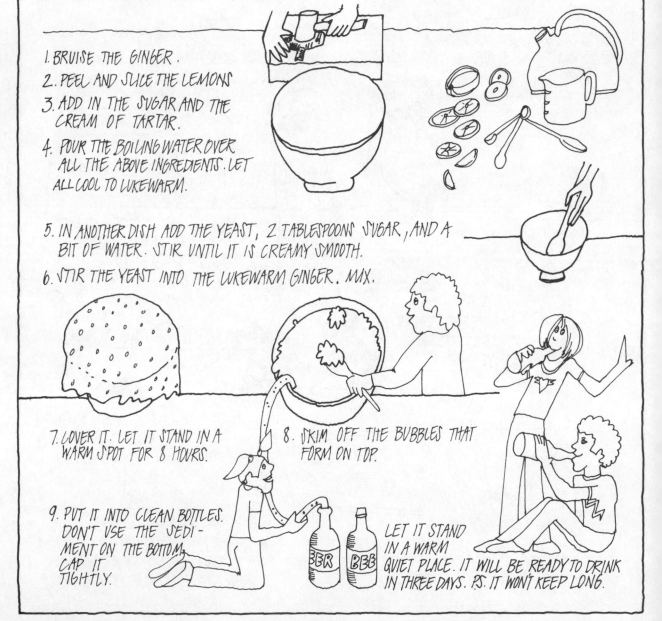

1. BRUISE THE GINGER.

2. PEEL AND SLICE THE LEMONS

3. ADD IN THE SUGAR AND THE CREAM OF TARTAR.

4. POUR THE BOILING WATER OVER ALL THE ABOVE INGREDIENTS. LET ALL COOL TO LUKEWARM.

5. IN ANOTHER DISH ADD THE YEAST, 2 TABLESPOONS SUGAR, AND A BIT OF WATER. STIR UNTIL IT IS CREAMY SMOOTH.

6. STIR THE YEAST INTO THE LUKEWARM GINGER. MIX.

7. COVER IT. LET IT STAND IN A WARM SPOT FOR 8 HOURS.

8. SKIM OFF THE BUBBLES THAT FORM ON TOP.

9. PUT IT INTO CLEAN BOTTLES. DON'T USE THE SEDIMENT ON THE BOTTOM. CAP IT TIGHTLY.

LET IT STAND IN A WARM QUIET PLACE. IT WILL BE READY TO DRINK IN THREE DAYS. P.S. IT WON'T KEEP LONG.

FINE FEATHERED FRIENDS

Feathers Are

Feathers are an extension of a bird's skin. Something like the hairs on your arms are an extension of your skin.

One purpose of feathers is to provide a lightweight, protective covering for bird bodies. Feathers are very good insulators because they are full of dead air spaces.

Birds have special muscles in their skin for fluffing out their feathers. You have those muscles too. They are the ones that give you goose bumps. Ever wonder why birds look fat on cold days?

Ancient Zipper

You probably have noticed that you can pull a feather apart and then close it again by running it between your fingers.

Birds have been zipping up ruffled feathers for 60,000,000 years. (And you thought zippers were a new invention!)

Hold a feather up to a strong light and look at it with a magnifying glass. See if you can see the hooks that form the locking mechanism.

Molt

Birds replace their feathers at least once a year. This is called molting. Usually it happens just after breeding season but it doesn't occur all at once. (Ever see a naked bird?) It happens gradually. Major feathers are lost symmetrically, one from each side, so that the bird can still fly.

Spring is the best time to collect feathers. Feathers have been prized as objects of art for a long time. Peruvians, Polynesians, and Victorian era ladies all decorated themselves with feathers.

Feather Puzzle

Take a look at your feather collection.

Every feather is different. Even if they were from the same bird that would be true. Feathers are fitted for a particular spot on the bird.

So what parts of the bird are your feathers from?

Wing feathers — are stiff on the forward side.

Tail feathers — are stiff along the middle.

Body feathers — are soft and downy.

Which side are your feathers from?

Hint: Birds, like people, are bilaterally symmetrical. So your feathers will be from either the right or the left side . . . if they are not from the middle, of course. Or from the top or bottom.

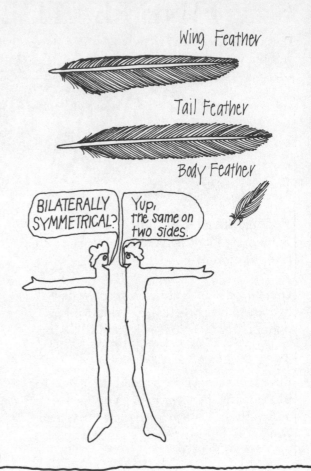

Colors from a Feather

You can get the tip of a feather to turn candlelight into colors. If conditions are right, you should see two or three ghost flames on either side of the real one, also bands of red and blue light. Try feathers from different birds.

Feather Decoration

Eskimos, Aztecs, Polynesians, Europeans, and American Indians all have worn feathers. And they all have worn them differently.

People often have rules for dressing. Sometimes the rules are written down and sometimes they are simply understood.

Men of the Blackfeet tribe wore eagle feathers in their hair. There were several ways to wear them. Each way had a different meaning. The number of red stripes painted on a feather told how many times the wearer had been wounded.

Feather Writing

For a long time quill pens were the only tools to write with. Follow the directions below and try your hand at some fancy penmanship.

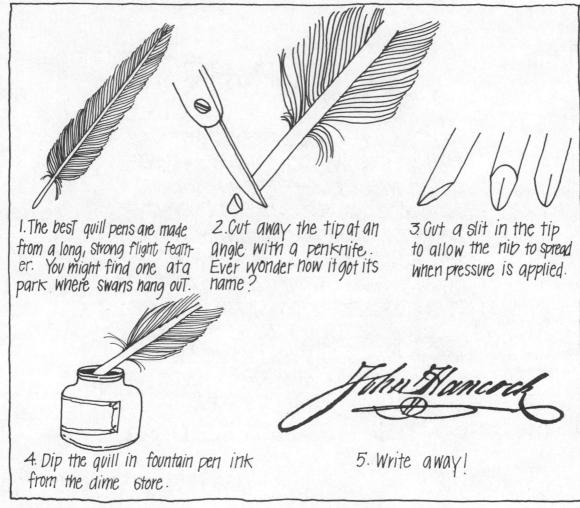

1. The best quill pens are made from a long, strong flight feather. You might find one at a park where swans hang out.

2. Cut away the tip at an angle with a penknife. Ever wonder how it got its name?

3. Cut a slit in the tip to allow the nib to spread when pressure is applied.

4. Dip the quill in fountain pen ink from the dime store.

5. Write away!

Drawing Pen

Try cutting different kinds of pen points on the tip of a feather after one wears out.

Rembrandt, who was a great "draughtsman," was fond of drawing with a quill pen. You might make some drawing pens. The library has books with Rembrandt's drawings in them. Look to see if the old master is good for some new ideas.

Invisible Ink

Use milk or lemon juice like ordinary ink. To read the invisible writing, hold the sheet next to a warm light bulb. The message will appear.

AUTUMN

DAYS SHRINK INTO LONGER NIGHTS. THE PURPLE MARTINS TAKE THEIR CUE AND START THEIR FLIGHT FROM MISSISSIPPI TO BRAZIL. WEEDS MAKE A QUICK COMEBACK, TAKING OVER RECENTLY-HARVESTED FIELDS. IT'S A GOOD TIME FOR INSECTS AND CATERPILLARS — UNTIL THE FIRST FROST. KIDS IN THE NORTHERN HEMISPHERE START BACK TO SCHOOL, WHILE KIDS "DOWN UNDER" LEAVE THEIR COATS BEHIND AND THINK ABOUT WHAT TO DO COME SUMMER.

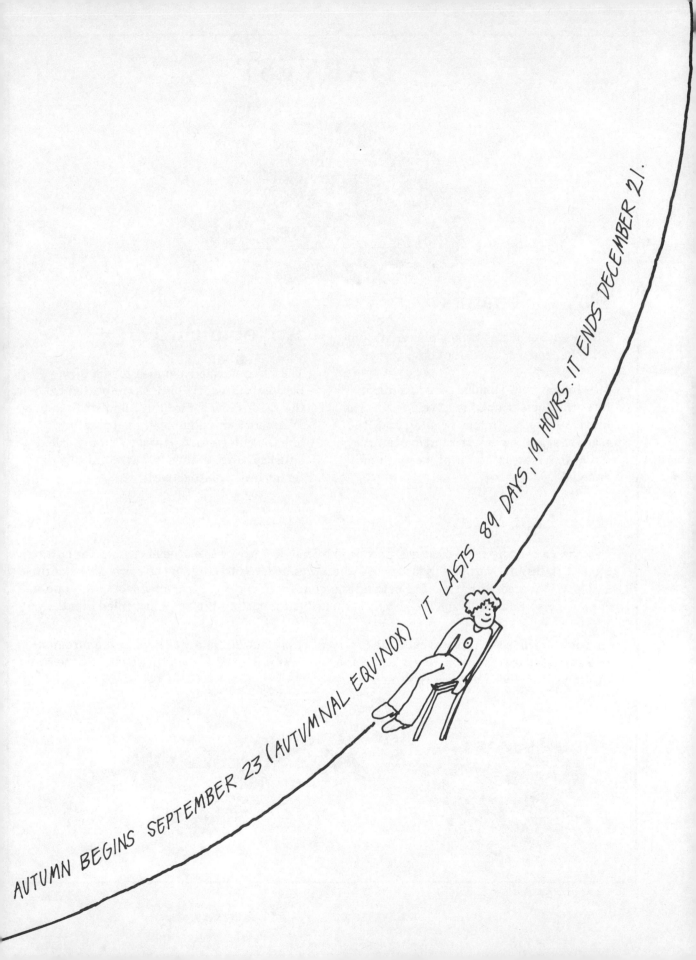

HARVEST

Day of Thanks

Thanksgiving means turkey dinner, a stomachache, and a whole lot of dirty dishes.

More than that, Thanksgiving commemorates the ancient holiday of celebrating the harvest. The Egyptians, Semites, and Romans may not have eaten turkey, but they did have a feast in honor of the earth mother's yield.

A Noble Bird

The English called a guinea fowl a *turkey* because this exotic bird was imported from the East. Since a bird the colonists found in America was a big feathered creature, like the guinea fowl, it was naturally called a turkey, even though it was a bird of a different feather altogether.

The Last Straw

Less than a century ago wheat was harvested by hand. There was a special custom for cutting the last stalks. In Europe this last bit of wheat was believed to contain the spirit of the corn and it was treated with care. In Scotland the youngest girl cut it. In some places everyone cut a little so no one person was totally responsible for cutting the last spirit-filled bundle.

In England the last sheaf was called the *maiden*, or *corn dollie*, and was kept in the farmhouse in a special place. This way the spirit of the corn was preserved for another year. At the end of the year the corn dollie was burned.

Kernel Corn

In order for a seed to form it must be pollinated. The male cell (pollen) of the plant must somehow get to the female parts (ovules or flowering parts).

A corn plant produces pollen at the top. It drops onto the corn tassels of the same or a neighboring plant. There is a tassel leading to every ovule.

Now, here comes the incredible part.

The pollen grain grows a tube down the center of the corn tassels until it reaches the ovule.

The pollen grain is about 1/1,000 of an inch. It grows a tube that might be as long as 12 inches. (Suppose you were a 5-foot pollen grain, you would have to grow a 12-mile tube to meet your ovule.)

Four Kinds of Corn

Flint corn, also called Indian corn, is the beautiful colored kind. The seeds are very hard.

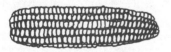

Dent corn has a dent in every seed. Along with flint corn it makes up most of the corn crop. They are used as cattle food.

Sweet corn is good eating corn, but you have to eat it soon after picking. After it's been picked the sugar begins to turn to starch. Within two days it's no longer sweet.

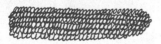

Popcorn is the seed that turns itself inside out. It has more water inside each seed than other corn. When you heat it the water explodes. Some kernels are duds. Three guesses why.

Corn Dance

The Seminole Indians of Florida celebrated the harvest each year with a festival. The celebration included preparing the stomach, by fasting and purging, for the ritual feast of maize.

The Natchez of Mississippi divided their year into thirteen moons. August was called *Moon of Maize* or *Great Corn*. It was the most important time of the year when the whole nation paid homage to the corn with feasts and games.

The Corn Spirit Lives

Each autumn ears of flint corn appear on people's doors, especially in the eastern United States.

Probably folks would be a little surprised if you knocked on their door and asked about the corn spirit.

It is a good way to welcome fall. It would be fun to try and find out how this custom got started.

Meanwhile, let corn color your door.

Find a couple of ears of Indian corn at a supermarket or fruit stand. If you can't find any there, look in a flower shop. Pick the prettiest ears you can find. Tie them together and tack them to your door.

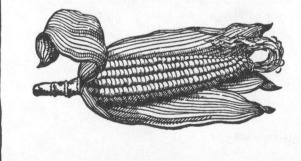

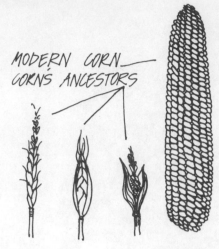

MODERN CORN
CORN'S ANCESTORS

Cereal of the Americas

All of our food plants have wild cousins. Ten thousand years of selective planting has changed a lot of vegetable faces. This change is called *domestication*.

Corn was grown at least 7,000 years ago by the Indians in South America. It is a kind of grass. You can see that by looking at its ancestors in the drawings.

Somehow, combining these three grasses and a lot of experimenting has produced the fat and sassy sweet corn we all know and love.

Now maize is a kind of plant freak. It has become dependent upon people for its survival. The handsome high-yield ears have seeds so tightly packed that they could never scatter and replant themselves, without a farmer's help.

---

corn - in England corn means "wheat," in Scotland corn means "oats," in America corn means "maize" — the yellow kernels that grow on a cob and taste great with melted butter. Corn, then, means the main cereal crop of a country.

Corn Husk Dolls

Dolls have an ancient history. Often they were representations made in great seriousness (more in the spirit of the corn dollie) and not at all used as playthings.

Corn husk dolls were made to be used as toys for Indian children by Indians in New England. It is thought that the Indians made them only after they saw the colonists' children carrying dolls.

YOU CAN MAKE CORN HUSK DOLLS WITH CORNHUSKS AND A BIT OF STRING.

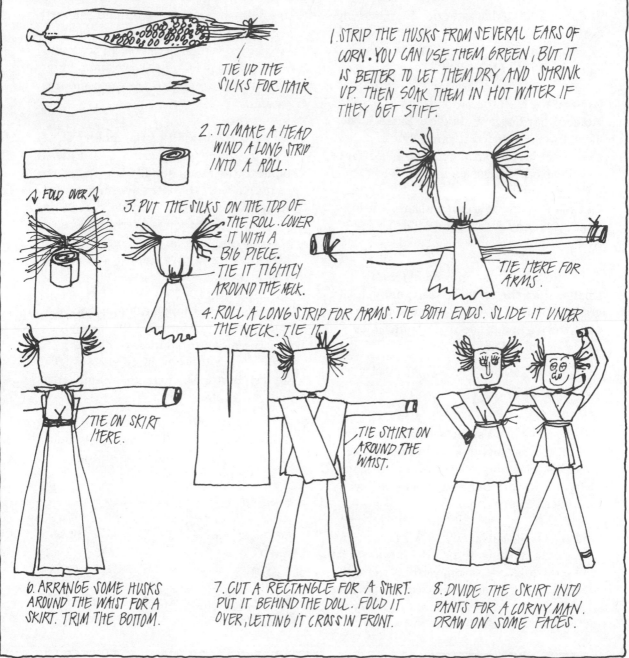

TIE UP THE SILKS FOR HAIR

1. STRIP THE HUSKS FROM SEVERAL EARS OF CORN. YOU CAN USE THEM GREEN, BUT IT IS BETTER TO LET THEM DRY AND SHRINK UP. THEN SOAK THEM IN HOT WATER IF THEY GET STIFF.

2. TO MAKE A HEAD WIND A LONG STRIP INTO A ROLL.

FOLD OVER

3. PUT THE SILKS ON THE TOP OF THE ROLL. COVER IT WITH A BIG PIECE. TIE IT TIGHTLY AROUND THE NECK.

TIE HERE FOR ARMS.

4. ROLL A LONG STRIP FOR ARMS. TIE BOTH ENDS. SLIDE IT UNDER THE NECK. TIE IT.

TIE ON SKIRT HERE.

TIE SHIRT ON AROUND THE WAIST.

6. ARRANGE SOME HUSKS AROUND THE WAIST FOR A SKIRT. TRIM THE BOTTOM.

7. CUT A RECTANGLE FOR A SHIRT. PUT IT BEHIND THE DOLL. FOLD IT OVER, LETTING IT CROSS IN FRONT.

8. DIVIDE THE SKIRT INTO PANTS FOR A CORNY MAN. DRAW ON SOME FACES.

MOON WATCH

Moon

The moon has a diameter one-fourth as big as the earth's. It orbits at a distance of thirty earth diameters and has a mass of one-eightieth that of the earth.

Next to the sun, the moon is the most obvious of our heavenly bodies. Earth folk have always watched it carefully. It imposes its rhythm on earth, and thus has affected all earth life since ancient times.

Our planet's moon is not ordinary. It is larger than any planetary satellite in our solar system.

Even though the moon is considerably smaller than the earth, it exerts enough gravitational force to move our seas. In fact, the earth and moon are sometimes called double planets.

Slow Moon

The moon's orbit speed seems to be slowing down. Scientists with atomic clocks have been keeping very careful time since 1955. They say our sister planet is decelerating at a very tiny rate.

This might be caused by tidal friction, but there is something more. The moon seems to be moving away from earth at the rate of about an inch a year. Scientists wonder if perhaps the universal force of gravity is getting weaker. Only time will tell.

Two-Planet System

To say the moon rotates around the earth is not exactly correct. Their mutual attraction causes the moon and earth to rotate around what is called a *barycenter*. It is the center of gravity of the earth-moon system.

Our tides are a result of the moon's strong attractive force. The earth's elastic seas respond to the moon's pull. The water heaps itself up a few feet as the moon moves along overhead. This happens twice a day — once when the moon is overhead, and again when the moon is on the direct opposite side of the earth. We call this time high tide.

The highest tide happens about once a month, when the sun and the moon line up. The moon provides seventy percent of the force; the sun thirty percent. Tides are seen best in shallow areas along large bodies of water.

WATER GETS HEAPED UP A FEW FEET UNDER THE MOON

Distance to the Moon

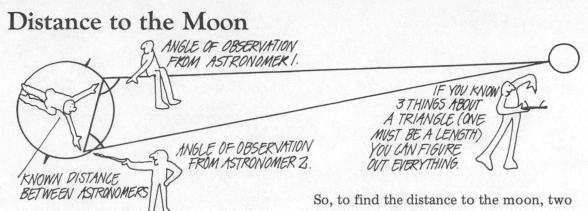

ANGLE OF OBSERVATION FROM ASTRONOMER 1.

IF YOU KNOW 3 THINGS ABOUT A TRIANGLE (ONE MUST BE A LENGTH) YOU CAN FIGURE OUT EVERYTHING.

ANGLE OF OBSERVATION FROM ASTRONOMER 2.

KNOWN DISTANCE BETWEEN ASTRONOMERS

You could travel to the moon to measure its distance from earth. But that's not a very practical way to measure, considering to get to the moon you need to know how much fuel it would take.

For a long time people have been answering difficult questions using a method called *deductive reasoning*. That's the method you use when you know two things and you shuffle them around in your mind to make them tell you a third thing.

So, to find the distance to the moon, two astronomers agree to site the moon at exactly the same time. The astronomers know the distance between each other, and they know the angles of observation of the moon.

Knowing these facts, figuring the moon's distance from earth is easy. Because the astronomers know that if you know three things about a triangle (in this case, the length of one side and the two angles of observation), then you know the size of the whole triangle.

Planetarium Eyes

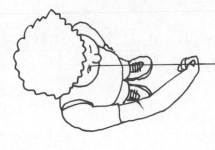

By pretending that your own eyes are planetariums you can get an idea of how this method of planet watching works.

Face a faraway object that you can see clearly. Hold out your arm, close one eye, and site down your arm so the object seems to rest on the end of your thumb.

Holding your arm very still, site with your other eye. Your thumb jumped even though you were holding it still. (You were holding it still, weren't you?)

The thumb jump means each eye sees the object at a different angle.

Moon Face

YOU CAN TELL WHAT PHASE THE MOON IS IN BY A QUICK DIRECTION CHECK OF ITS CUSPS OR HORNS. ALSO THERE ARE SOME SPECIAL MOONS TO WATCH.

<u>WAXING MOON</u> (FIRST QUARTER) THE HORNS POINTING LEFT MEAN IT IS APPROACHING THE FULL MOON.

<u>WANING MOON</u> (THIRD QUARTER) THE HORNS POINTING RIGHT MEAN IT IS APPROACHING THE NEW MOON.

<u>HARVEST MOON</u> (FIRST FULL MOON AFTER AUTUMNAL EQUINOX) THIS LARGE ORANGE MOON SEEMS TO HANG ABOVE THE HORIZON, BECAUSE IT RISES ALONG THE HORIZON, INSTEAD OF STRAIGHT UP. IT IS NAMED HARVEST MOON BECAUSE IT RISES ABOUT THE TIME THE SUN SETS. THE EXTRA LIGHT HELPS FARMERS TO GATHER CROPS.

<u>HUNTER'S MOON</u> (THE FULL MOON FOLLOWING THE HARVEST MOON) IT IS ALMOST AS BRIGHT, BUT NOT QUITE. THE STRANGE ORANGE COLOR IS DUE TO THE FACT WE SEE IT THROUGH THE DENSE ATMOSPHERE ALONG THE HORIZON.

<u>BLUE MOON</u> THE RARE OCCURRENCE OF TWO FULL MOONS FALLING IN THE SAME CALENDAR MONTH.

Loony

Police records show that crimes are more numerous during days of the full moon.

Hospital records seem to show that bleeding increases during the full moon.

There is some evidence that great storms in history have been influenced by the lunar cycle.

People who are a little crazy are said to become crazier during periods of the full moon.

Ever wonder where the word *lunatic* came from?

A Wealth of Information in *Poor Richard's*

A serious sky watcher should have an almanac. It contains all sorts of valuable information, like rising and setting times of the sun (so you'll know exactly what *be home before dark* means).

It has phases of the moon, times of high and low tides, and information about the planets and stars. It also has a list of special events, like eclipses and meteor showers, and holidays you didn't even know existed. You can buy all this information and more for less than a dollar.

SPORE LORE

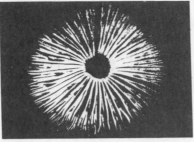

Spore Prints

To make a spore print, remove the stem from a ripe mushroom and place the mushroom head face down on a sheet of paper. Try both dark and light paper because mushrooms make different colored spores.

What's a Fungus Anyway?

About one-tenth of the world's plants are called *fungi* (which is the plural of *fungus*). They contain no chlorophyll, so they can't convert sunlight directly to food. They make their living by feeding on dead things or on other organisms.

There are all kinds of fungi — smuts, molds, yeasts, and mushrooms. They are at home in many places, like under floors and between your toes. They are all made of tiny hair-like structures called *hyphae*. Some are simple, like the ones that grow on old bread; some are more complex, like mushrooms. Many make spores.

sporadic - means happening occasionally. (Like the chances of a spore's survival are hit or miss.)

So What's a Spore For?

Spores are the seeds of fungi. They are much smaller and simpler than seeds. They are also much less equipped to survive, so a fungus makes up for a high fatality rate by producing a huge number of spores.

A mushroom is the spore-making part of a vast network of hyphae. Its job is to produce spores. A large mushroom could drop 10,000 spores a second and this could go on for 7 days.

Spore Rain

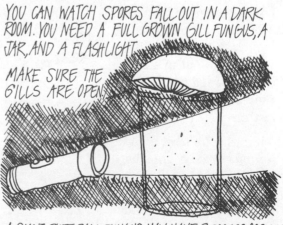

YOU CAN WATCH SPORES FALL OUT IN A DARK ROOM. YOU NEED A FULL GROWN GILL FUNGUS, A JAR, AND A FLASHLIGHT.

MAKE SURE THE GILLS ARE OPEN.

A GIANT PUFF BALL FUNGUS MAY HAVE 2,000,000,000,000 SPORES. LUCKILY, ONLY A FEW WILL GROW.

Spore Guns

GILL MUSHROOM

SINGLE GILL ENLARGED

GILL WALL

SPORE GUN (BASIDIOSPORE)

WHEN A GILL IS TILTED, THE SPORES CAN'T FALL OUT.

EACH "GUN" IS LOADED WITH FOUR SPORES. WHEN RIPE, THEY SHOOT OFF AND DROP TO THE GROUND.

Spores must find their way into the moving air layer just above the ground if they expect to get anywhere. Fungi grow some amazing devices for launching spores. The puff ball, a type of fungus, is like a big bag that belches spores when poked by rain.

Gill fungi have a sort of spore gun that shoots spores from its gill walls. The guns are very accurate, shooting spores to half the distance between the gills. Then, from a spore's point of view, it's rather like falling through a long tunnel. In order for the free fall to work, the gills must be exactly vertical to gravity.

Mushrooms are very sensitive to gravity and will adjust themselves, even to the point of growing gills on top of their umbrellas, if they are upset.

The Magic Mushroom

Mushrooms have often been associated with magic in people's minds.

Strange Tales of Amanita Muscaria (Also Known as "Fly Agaric")

This mushroom is used in eastern Europe as a fly killer. It is put in a bowl of sweetened milk. For flies who imbibe, it's their last meal.

Vikings took a bit of *Amanita muscaria* before a battle. Its effect was one of intoxication, and a feeling that nothing could stop them. They were known as *berserkers*.

A Morel Story

A *morel* is another member of the fungus family. According to an old tale, the devil, who was in bad temper, met an old woman in the wood. He seized her and cut her into bits and threw the pieces about the wood. From these pieces sprang up morels.

THE BUG

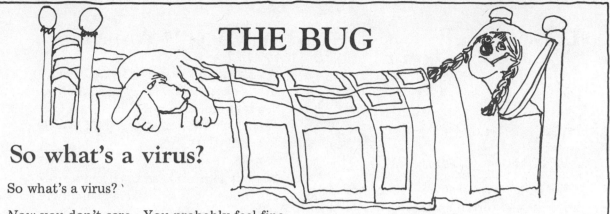

So what's a virus?

So what's a virus? '

Now you don't care. You probably feel fine.

Stop! Save this page for those days in bed when you have nothing else to do. Those days when you've got *it*. Or it's got you.

Okay. You've got a headache. Your body sort of hurts, and maybe your stomach aches and you wish you didn't feel like a truck ran over you. Today even school looks like fun.

That's it! You've got a virus — or the symptoms of a virus.

Your doctor might have given you the once-over and after a few thumps and pokes said, "Well, it's probably the bug (that's a nickname for a virus)."

Somehow you got the feeling he wasn't too sure of what he was talking about. That's true. But until recently no one knew much about viruses. Even now it's hard to say whether they're dead or alive.

Class Struggle

A virus — dead or alive?

A simple question, with a not very simple answer. Perhaps some of the problem is the question.

People like to order things. They like to think of the universe in nice neat classes. Animal, mineral, vegetable. Up or down. Dead or alive.

There *is* an order to things in the universe; it's just that they don't fall into neat little packages. Fish fly, mammals lay eggs, molds crawl, crystals grow. The trick is to consider the subject first, and its class last.

While you are in bed you might want to play a game of "animal, mineral, vegetable." If you come to virus — you might have to think of a new game.

Other Ways to Be Sick

IF THIS → . WERE A POLIO VIRUS, THEN

THIS → ● WOULD BE AN INFLUENZA VIRUS AND 10 TIMES THIS CIRCLE EQUALS THE SIZE OF A RED BLOOD CELL. (500 LIFE-SIZE RED BLOOD CELLS WOULD FILL A PERIOD ON THIS PAGE.)

Viruses are by no means the cause of all your ills. There are a host of other ways to be sick. There are bacteria, rikitssia, plain old poisons, and mechanical failures (like a broken arm).

But viruses do cause measles, mumps, chicken pox, anthrax, yellow fever, influenza, not to mention the common cold.

This Is a Cell

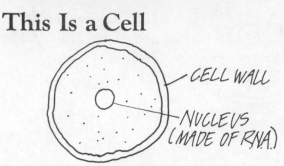

It can do all sorts of things. It can take in nutrients and turn them into cell material (protoplasm). It might live alone or with a group of other cells in a body. Every cell that lives in a body commune has a specialized job. It might carry oxygen, make the body move (muscle), provide cover (skin), or carry messages (nerves).

The nucleus is the cell center. It is the headquarters of the cell. It stores information and directs all cell operations. It's made of RNA (ribonucleic acid) which is the blueprint for all cell activity.

Wandering Nucleic Acid Blueprint

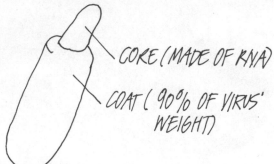

This is a virus. It is not a cell.

A virus has a protein coat, which is ninety-five percent of its weight, and an RNA core.

A virus is a nucleus with its coat on. It wanders around until it can find a cell to get its core into.

A Virus Is Amazing

A virus has no means of locomotion. It doesn't eat. It cannot grow, although it can reproduce. A virus can look like a crystal and be stored on a shelf in a jar like salt.

When it gets inside an organism a virus can suddenly behave like a living thing. It can invade a cell and make hundreds of copies of itself. And it can mutate, which means that its copies can adjust themselves to a new environment, making a virus very hard to kill — if it were alive in the first place.

Immunity

Immunity means the right antibodies are circulating in your blood. They are ready to kill germ invaders quickly — before the villains can multiply.

In a lifetime a body reacts to something like 100,000 different antigens (substances that stimulate the body to produce an antibody).

You already have many antibodies in your body when you are born. New ones are created when you are vaccinated.

The first vaccine was made from cowpox virus from a cow. In fact, the word "vaccine" comes from the Latin word for cow — *vacca*.

Incredible Battle

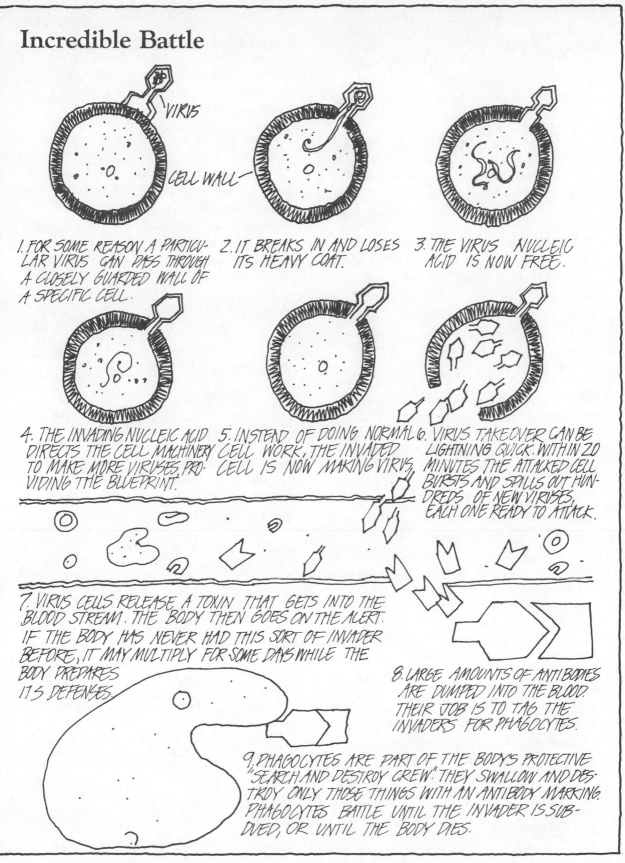

VIRUS

CELL WALL

1. FOR SOME REASON A PARTICULAR VIRUS CAN PASS THROUGH A CLOSELY GUARDED WALL OF A SPECIFIC CELL.

2. IT BREAKS IN AND LOSES ITS HEAVY COAT.

3. THE VIRUS NUCLEIC ACID IS NOW FREE.

4. THE INVADING NUCLEIC ACID DIRECTS THE CELL MACHINERY TO MAKE MORE VIRUSES, PROVIDING THE BLUEPRINT.

5. INSTEAD OF DOING NORMAL CELL WORK, THE INVADED CELL IS NOW MAKING VIRUS.

6. VIRUS TAKE OVER CAN BE LIGHTNING QUICK. WITHIN 20 MINUTES THE ATTACKED CELL BURSTS AND SPILLS OUT HUNDREDS OF NEW VIRUSES, EACH ONE READY TO ATTACK.

7. VIRUS CELLS RELEASE A TOXIN THAT GETS INTO THE BLOOD STREAM. THE BODY THEN GOES ON THE ALERT. IF THE BODY HAS NEVER HAD THIS SORT OF INVADER BEFORE, IT MAY MULTIPLY FOR SOME DAYS WHILE THE BODY PREPARES ITS DEFENSES.

8. LARGE AMOUNTS OF ANTIBODIES ARE DUMPED INTO THE BLOOD. THEIR JOB IS TO TAG THE INVADERS FOR PHAGOCYTES.

9. PHAGOCYTES ARE PART OF THE BODY'S PROTECTIVE "SEARCH AND DESTROY CREW." THEY SWALLOW AND DESTROY ONLY THOSE THINGS WITH AN ANTIBODY MARKING. PHAGOCYTES BATTLE UNTIL THE INVADER IS SUBDUED, OR UNTIL THE BODY DIES.

Cold Season

It seems as though colds come in seasons. A summer cold doesn't feel as miserable as a winter cold. It might be interesting to start a chart of who gets sick when in your family, to see if any pattern emerges.

People who live in isolated places usually lead cold-free lives. They develop a resistance to local infections. Island dwellers, who have little contact with the outside world, have noted that after a foreign ship has landed and departed from their shores, it leaves the local folk with a lot of sore throats and runny noses.

Infections spread through a population. Usually they are an equal match for body defenses. But when a particularly nasty infection arrives, for which a population's defenses are too weak, an epidemic occurs.

In 1918 a worldwide epidemic occurred. Influenza struck Europe and attacked both young and old, both weak and strong. It moved to America, then to China, Russia, Asia, and Australia. In one year 10 to 20 million people died of this virus or its complications.

Since then the flu epidemic struck in 1957 and 1966. We are now better prepared with antibiotics (drugs like penicillin) to fight an epidemic.

Also, the World Health Organization keeps a sort of worldwide infection watch, on a constant alert for vicious new infections. They operate a tracking and warning system, much as the weather bureau keeps tabs on hurricanes, cyclones, and other natural disasters.

Get Lotsa Rest

The next time you are sick, have a friend get a book out of the library about the first vaccine and the amazing search for the invisible virus.

There will be a chapter about Dr. Edward Jenner and how he tested the vaccine, and how the kid he tested it on lived and is the secret hero. It's better than any TV war story and it's a real story about the competition for life. Life is a contest to exist. You are running in the contest — whether you know it or not.

P.S.   Get well soon.

Sense Test

It can be interesting to test your taster and see if it's making any sense while you are sick with a stuffed-up nose.

Have a friend make up a tray of different tastes: sweet, sour, salty, hot. You should take this test blindfolded, so there are no visual hints.

Which tastes are on your tongue, and which ones does your nose know?

CHUNKS OF RAW POTATO, ONION, APPLE, TURNIP, OR PARSNIP. PEEL THEM SO THERE ARE NO HINTS.

CRYSTAL CLEAR

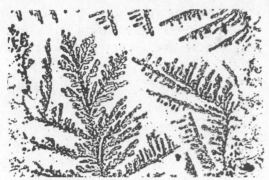
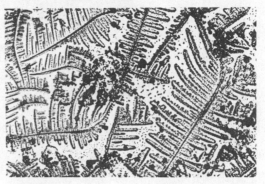

Can Dead Things Grow?

Growing means getting bigger. Kittens grow into cats, small boys grow into big ball players, and tadpoles grow into frogs.

The sort of growing you do is called *development*. It means a creature starts out in one shape and over a period of time it eats, breaks down food, and grows up.

Crystals grow too, but in a different way. They make an orderly change from small to large, but they don't develop the way living things do.

A crystal is made of atoms. So are you. Your atoms are organized into cells, and cells grow by breaking down nutrients and turning them into cell material (protoplasm). Cells grow from the inside. Crystals grow from the outside by adding atoms to their surface.

Crystal Garden

Here is a simple way to grow crystals of your own.

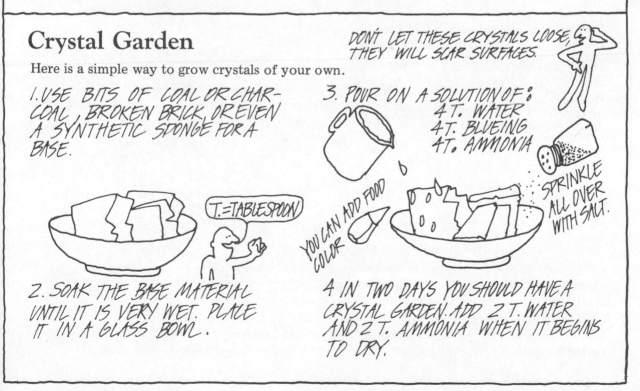

DON'T LET THESE CRYSTALS LOOSE, THEY WILL SCAR SURFACES.

1. USE BITS OF COAL OR CHARCOAL, BROKEN BRICK, OR EVEN A SYNTHETIC SPONGE FOR A BASE.

T.=TABLESPOON

2. SOAK THE BASE MATERIAL UNTIL IT IS VERY WET. PLACE IT IN A GLASS BOWL.

3. POUR ON A SOLUTION OF:
4 T. WATER
4 T. BLUEING
4 T. AMMONIA

YOU CAN ADD FOOD COLOR

SPRINKLE ALL OVER WITH SALT.

4 IN TWO DAYS YOU SHOULD HAVE A CRYSTAL GARDEN. ADD 2 T. WATER AND 2 T. AMMONIA WHEN IT BEGINS TO DRY.

Atoms

Atoms are elemental particles, the building blocks of nature. Atoms are all that matter is.

Atoms used to be thought of as the tiniest particles possible. Alas, now we know that they are just a step down along the way to small. When atoms are squeezed and smashed we find they are made of even smaller, though still mysterious, particles.

Atoms are attractive. They come together to make molecules. Some molecules are small and simple, like water (two hydrogens and an oxygen), or salt (a sodium and a chlorine).

Some molecules are bigger and made in more cunning ways, like proteins and protoplasm — the stuff of flesh and blood, and orchids and rutabagas.

All That Matters
(or, Crystal Theory)

Molecules make up matter, which comes in three classes: solids, liquids, and gasses.

In a gas, molecules move about freely, although they often collide.

In liquids, molecules are more attracted to each other and they wander less freely.

In solids, molecules are stuck with their neighbors.

Some solids are special. Their molecules pack up in a very orderly way. This order is repeated throughout the substance and gives it a special shape. These solids are called *crystals*.

Crystal Theory

You can demonstrate crystal theory to yourself with a bag of marbles and a cake pan. Think of the marbles as atoms or molecules.

A *gas* is like having only a few marbles. The marbles (atoms) are moving rapidly.

A *liquid* is sort of like having more marbles in your pan. They move at a slower speed.

A *solid* is having as many marbles packed together as will fit into the pan space. They won't be able to move much, even if they wanted to.

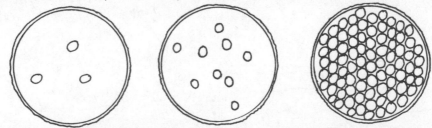

Notice the pattern the marbles form when they're crowded. A real crystal has depth. Instead of each atom having 6 neighbors, like in the pan, it would have 12.

Stir the marbles well. What was a careful order before will form irregularities, or vacancies. Now pack the marbles tightly again. Push a marble into the center of your *crystal structure*. What happens? Who moves over? Where? What happens in a real crystal?

Grow Your Own

Even though its growth seems slow, a crystal grows at a fantastic speed. If you could watch it grow you would see something like 16 million, million, million atoms rushing to line up across a crystal face every hour. That is a lot of atoms (it is something like the number of sand grains in a cubic mile of beach).

It's not surprising that in this mad growth scramble there is occasionally a mistake. Perhaps an impurity slips in or a vacancy occurs or a line gets out of place. In fact, in nature a perfect crystal is a great rarity.

But no matter how odd crystals might look, they do remain true to their crystal form. Someone wrote a law about crystals called the *law of constancy of angle*. In all crystals of the same substance the angles between corresponding faces remain the same.

Crystal Gazing

You most likely already have a good collection of crystals around the house. Sort your kitchen crystal collection into groups according to shape. You might need a magnifying glass since some of the crystals will be rather small.

ice - scrape the crystals from the freezer compartment of your refrigerator.

salt - (rock salt would be better)

sugar

washing soda

epsom salt

Rock Candy Mountain

You can watch crystals grow and then eat the results. Make rock candy crystals!

SOME CRYSTAL GROWERS GENTLY TAP THEIR GLASS

GROW CRYSTALS ON A STICK FOR ROCK LOLLIPOPS.

1. PUT ½ CUP OF WATER INTO A PAN. ADD 1 CUP OF SUGAR. HEAT IT OVER A LOW FLAME UNTIL THE SUGAR DISSOLVES. DO NOT STIR. LET IT BOIL FOR 1 MINUTE.

2. POUR THE WARM SYRUP INTO A GLASS. HANG A WEIGHTED STRING INTO THE SYRUP. LET IT STAND AT ROOM TEMPERATURE.

3. LARGE CRYSTALS WILL BEGIN TO FORM IN ABOUT A WEEK. YOU MAY NEED TO BREAK THE CRUST TO KEEP THE WATER EVAPORATING.

Paper Pack

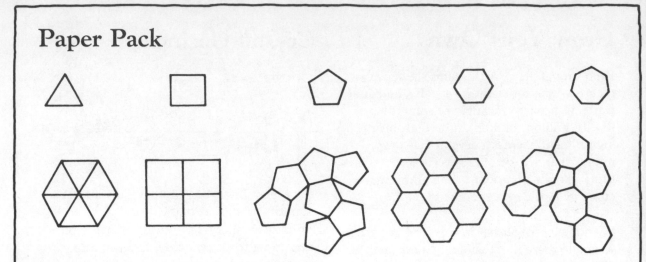

Just what makes a good crystal shape?

Here is a packing experiment. Cut some of each of the above shapes out of heavy paper. How many ways will a triangle stack? How tightly will a triangle pack? Try stacking and packing the rest of the shapes. Now mix the shapes. Remember, the object is to put the shapes as close together as possible. Different atoms or molecules generally have different shapes. In order to grow a good crystal you usually need a pure material.

Because the atoms of crystals have varied shapes, they will pack and form a crystal that reflects their particular shape. Their insides look like their outsides. You can identify a crystal by its shape.

Minerals
(or, All That Glitters Is Not Gold.)

Ever pick up a rock because you took a shine to it?

What may have caught your eye was its sparkle. If you looked closely, your new-found rock may have had tiny crystals that acted like mini-mirrors reflecting light.

Naturally-occurring crystals are called *minerals*. They are formed from the seas, and they come from *magma* (molten matter under the earth's crust) cooling, evaporating, and coming out from under pressure. They range from microscopic to gigantic. They come in many colors, shapes, and sizes.

Crystal Clear

Most solids are opaque (they won't let light through).

But many crystals, because of their orderly atomic structure, allow light beams to pass through their very solid structure and come out on the other side. They are transparent.

WHERE THERE'S LIFE THERE'S GRASS

Grass for Breakfast

Cereals are seeds. Seeds from different kinds of grasses. Wheat, oats, corn, barley, rye, and rice are all grasses. Even sugar cane is a grass.

Someone once said that all great civilizations have grown up on a cereal of some sort.

Two-thirds of the world's population depends on the grass family for its main diet. One-fourth of the food eaten in America is cereal.

Let Them Eat Cake

A cow must eat more than 21 pounds of grain to produce a pound of steak. Thus, more people can be fed directly from an acre of land planted with grain than they can by eating cattle fed on the same amount of land. Ever wonder why buns are cheaper than burgers?

What's So Special about Grass?

An important fact about grass is that you can cut off its head and it won't die. In fact, it is hardly set back. A good trick to know when you live in a world full of grazers.

Gramineae, or members of the grass family, cover the earth. That in itself is very important, for without grass, soil erosion would be tremendous.

More important than that, grass provides food directly to humans in the form of cereals and, indirectly, in the form of lamb chops and hamburgers.

Cows eat grass. It is probably in this way that grasses evolved their talent for living without heads — a way of surviving alongside grazing animals.

Grass's secret for living without a head lies in the fact that it is mostly a leaf. In most plants growing takes place at the tips of the shoots. When you lop off the top, the plant takes a long time to recover. With a grass, new tissue grows from its base. So when you cut off the top, the grass grows on. Think about this phenomenon the next time you mow the lawn.

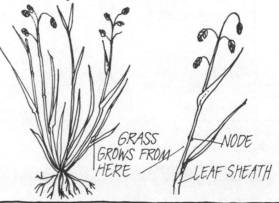

GRASS GROWS FROM HERE — NODE — LEAF SHEATH

Breakfast of Romans

Frumenty is a breakfast cereal that Romans used to eat. The main ingredient is whole wheat kernels. You could try and buy some wheat from your local farmer or feed store. Make sure it hasn't been sprayed. City folks should try to buy it at a health food shop.

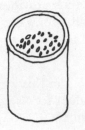 

1. FILL AN OVEN-PROOF JAR 3/4 FULL OF WHEAT GRAINS.

2. FILL THE JAR TO THE TOP WITH WATER.

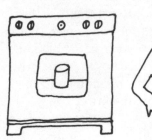 

3. LET IT STAND IN A WARM OVEN (200°) FOR 10-12 HOURS UNTIL ALL THE GRAINS BURST.

4. EAT IT HOT OR COLD WITH MILK AND SUGAR.

cereal - comes from the word *cerelia*, harvest festival of the Romans honoring the grain goddess, Ceres.

Grass Whistle

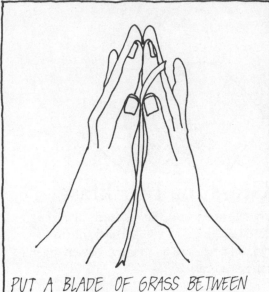

PUT A BLADE OF GRASS BETWEEN YOUR THUMBS AND BLOW THROUGH THE SPACE YOUR THUMBS MAKE. IT DOESN'T MATTER WHAT THE REST OF YOUR FINGERS DO. ADJUST THE TENSION FOR A BETTER SOUND.

Fibers

After food, fibers are the best gift to us from the plant world.

We write on fibers, wrap garbage in fibers, keep warm wearing fibers, climb mountains with ropes of fibers, paint on fibers, and bind things with fibers. We have explored the earth under sails made from fibers.

Fibers come from a wide range of plants. Cotton is the first to come to mind. But people also use fibers from flax, nettles, cactus, and cannabis (also known as hemp).

There is a project in this book that tells you how to use the fibers in plain old lawn grass to make paper.

Grass Flowers

Yes, grasses do have flowers. Not the big, showy kind with loud colors and heavy scents. Grasses don't need to have those kinds of attracting devices. The wind carries their pollen so they don't have to compete for insects' attention.

The heads of grasses, even though they are the plain janes of the flower world, can be beautiful. It might be fun to start a collection of the grasses in your neighborhood.

There are more than 700 kinds in the world. Certainly they're not all on your block, or even in your latitude, but there should be enough to get you started on becoming a local grass expert.

GRASS FLOWER

"FLOWER" FLOWER

Head Collection

ONE WAY TO COLLECT GRASSES IS BY MAKING A PHOTOGRAPHIC PRINT OF THEM. YOU WILL NEED A PACKAGE OF PHOTOGRAPHIC PROOF PAPER F (ALSO CALLED CONTACT PRINTING OUT PAPER), A BOX OF FIXER (SODIUM THIOSULFATE), A SHEET OF GLASS, AND SOME GRASSES.

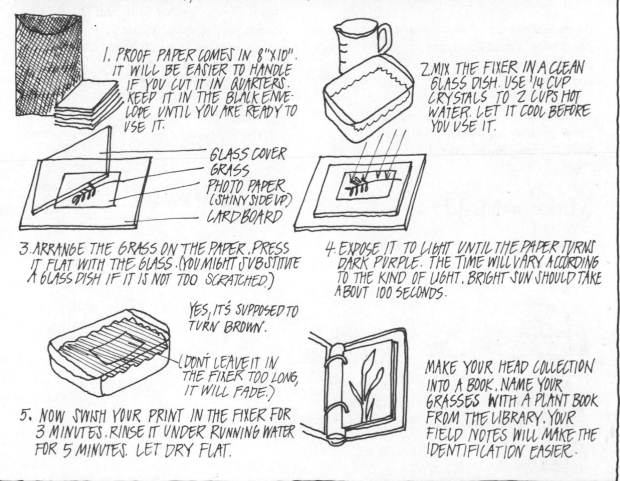

1. PROOF PAPER COMES IN 8"X10". IT WILL BE EASIER TO HANDLE IF YOU CUT IT IN QUARTERS. KEEP IT IN THE BLACK ENVELOPE UNTIL YOU ARE READY TO USE IT.

GLASS COVER
GRASS
PHOTO PAPER (SHINY SIDE UP)
CARDBOARD

2. MIX THE FIXER IN A CLEAN GLASS DISH. USE 1/4 CUP CRYSTALS TO 2 CUPS HOT WATER. LET IT COOL BEFORE YOU USE IT.

3. ARRANGE THE GRASS ON THE PAPER. PRESS IT FLAT WITH THE GLASS. (YOU MIGHT SUBSTITUTE A GLASS DISH IF IT IS NOT TOO SCRATCHED.)

4. EXPOSE IT TO LIGHT UNTIL THE PAPER TURNS DARK PURPLE. THE TIME WILL VARY ACCORDING TO THE KIND OF LIGHT. BRIGHT SUN SHOULD TAKE ABOUT 100 SECONDS.

YES, IT'S SUPPOSED TO TURN BROWN.

(DON'T LEAVE IT IN THE FIXER TOO LONG, IT WILL FADE.)

5. NOW SWISH YOUR PRINT IN THE FIXER FOR 3 MINUTES. RINSE IT UNDER RUNNING WATER FOR 5 MINUTES. LET DRY FLAT.

MAKE YOUR HEAD COLLECTION INTO A BOOK. NAME YOUR GRASSES WITH A PLANT BOOK FROM THE LIBRARY. YOUR FIELD NOTES WILL MAKE THE IDENTIFICATION EASIER.

PAPERWORKS

Paper's Past

Before paper, people wrote on rocks, clay tablets, and animal skins. The Romans sometimes wrote on palmyra leaves. They put holes in them and strung them into a kind of book. Three guesses why modern pages are called *leaves*.

Papermaking

Paper is something we use a lot, but we don't give it much thought. Here are some papermaking secrets so you can try making paper yourself.

Autumn is the best time to harvest plants for papermaking because the plant fibres have become tough over the summer.

Paper was invented by the Chinese about 105 A.D. According to legend, T'sai Lung, a court scribe, made paper from bark, rags, and fish net in order to please the emperor, who was tired of writing on silk. China carefully guarded the papermaking secret for 500 years. Then like all great inventions the recipe leaked out and was later carried to the West along the great caravan routes.

Paper has come a long way. Once a rare and royal stuff, now it wraps your trash.

Make a Mold

To make paper there are three basic steps. You have to make a mold. You must make a fiber pulp. And you have to get the pulp into the mold.

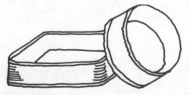

1. MAKE A MOLD USING A TIN CAN WITH SHORT SIDES, LIKE A TUNA OR SARDINE CAN. THE SHAPE OF THE CAN MAKES THE SHAPE OF THE PAPER.

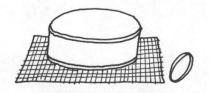

2. CUT OUT THE TOP AND BOTTOM. CUT A PIECE OF CHEESE CLOTH BIG ENOUGH TO COVER ONE END OF THE CAN.

3. STRETCH THE CLOTH OVER ONE END. FASTEN IT WITH A RUBBER BAND. SMOOTH OUT THE WRINKLES, AND MAKE IT TIGHT.

Make Pulp

BEFORE YOU BEGIN, HAVE MOM OR DAD BUY SOME CAUSTIC SODA. IT IS A CHEMICAL THEY USE TO CLEAN PIPES. IT CAN BE <u>VERY DANGEROUS</u>, SO LET THEM HANDLE IT!

NEXT, CUT YOUR FIBERS. ORDINARY LAWN GRASS WILL DO. CHOOSE THE GRASS THAT GROWS AROUND TREES AND NEXT TO FENCES, WHERE THE MOWER NEVER GOES. THAT'S THE GRASS THAT'S THE OLDEST AND TOUGHEST. LATER ON YOU CAN EXPERIMENT WITH OTHER PLANTS LIKE CATTAILS, LARGE SHAGGY WEEDS, AND STALKS— WHATEVER MAKES PULP.

1. CUT UP SEVERAL LARGE HANDFULS OF GRASS INTO A LARGE POTTERY BOWL.

2. COVER THE GRASS WITH BOILING WATER. HAVE AN ADULT POUR IN 6-8 TEASPOONS OF CAUSTIC SODA. LET IT SIT OVERNIGHT IN A SAFE PLACE.

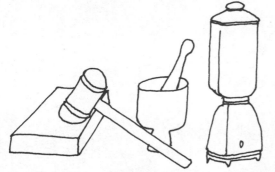

3. YOU HAVE TO BREAK UP THE FIBERS SOMEHOW. USE A BLENDER, PESTLE, OR A BREADBOARD AND CROQUET MALLET. BEAT THOSE FIBERS!

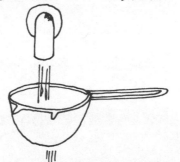

4. WHEN YOU HAVE A FINE PULPY MASS, MASH IT IN A STRAINER. IT SHOULDN'T FEEL SLIPPERY OR LUMPY. IF IT DOES, TAKE IT BACK FOR ANOTHER BEATING.

Mold It

TRY TO GET THE FIBERS ONTO THE MOLD EVENLY. IT WILL TAKE A BIT OF PRACTICE. DON'T FORGET TO JIGGLE ; THIS WILL GIVE YOUR PAPER EXTRA STRENGTH.

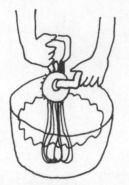  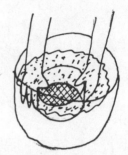

1. PUT YOUR FIBERS INTO A BOWL FULL OF WATER. GIVE THEM A WHIRL WITH A BEATER SO THEY ARE WELL SEPARATED.

2. PUT THE MOLD INTO THE BOWL. TRY NOT TO CATCH ANY FIBERS ON THE WAY DOWN.

3. LIFT THE MOLD, CATCHING A FILM OF FIBERS ON THE SCREEN. TRY TO MAKE THEM AS EVEN AS POSSIBLE.

Peel It

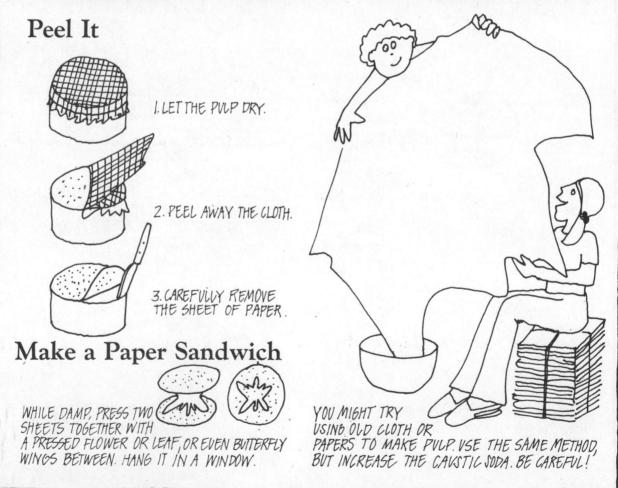

1. LET THE PULP DRY.

2. PEEL AWAY THE CLOTH.

3. CAREFULLY REMOVE THE SHEET OF PAPER.

Make a Paper Sandwich

WHILE DAMP, PRESS TWO SHEETS TOGETHER WITH A PRESSED FLOWER OR LEAF, OR EVEN BUTTERFLY WINGS BETWEEN. HANG IT IN A WINDOW.

YOU MIGHT TRY USING OLD CLOTH OR PAPERS TO MAKE PULP. USE THE SAME METHOD, BUT INCREASE THE CAUSTIC SODA. BE CAREFUL!

ALL HALLOWS' EVE

Halloween

By now you probably know that if you scratch the surface of a holiday, you are likely to find it was once a celebration of quite another kind. Halloween is an ancient feast with another face.

In the early religion of Ireland and Scotland, *Samhain*, November 1, was New Year's Day. It was the time when the gods of light and darkness were honored. Old fires were allowed to die and new ones were lit.

It was a time spirits came back to visit the living and it was a time for prying into the unknown. Divinations were performed to find out who you were to marry, or who was soon to die.

Christians put the feast of All Souls on this day and it became the Christian time to remember the dead. Superstitious (non-Christian) behavior was discouraged, but the spirit of Halloween lived on.

Dress Up Night

Some people think that dressing in costume on Halloween comes from an old Celtic custom. With all those spirits of the departed around at New Year's, they were certain to be at the feast. Villagers masked themselves and led the ghosts to the city limits after dinner. A polite way of disposing of dinner guests.

Trick or Treat

In America, around the turn of the century, the night before Halloween used to be known as Mischief Night.

All sorts of shenanigans went on then. Windows were soaped, outhouses overturned, belongings misplaced — and it all could be blamed on bad fairies.

Make a Voice Disguiser

Here is a simple device to make for some of your own Halloween shenanigans.

You need a paper tube, a square of wax paper, and a rubber band.

CUT A SLIT HERE

1. PULL THE PAPER TIGHTLY OVER ONE END. FASTEN IT WITH A RUBBER BAND.

2. PRESS OPEN THE SLIT. TALK THROUGH THE OPEN END.

Halloween - All Hallows' Eve, or holy evening; the night before All Saints' Day.

Do Your Worst, Mangel-Wurzel

Fire was once thought to frighten witches. One method of scaring witches was to leave out mangel-wurzels (a root, kind of like a beet or turnip). They were left in a place where witches and spirits would be sure to see them. (When the Celts came to America they substituted native pumpkins for turnips, and the jack-o'-lantern was born.)

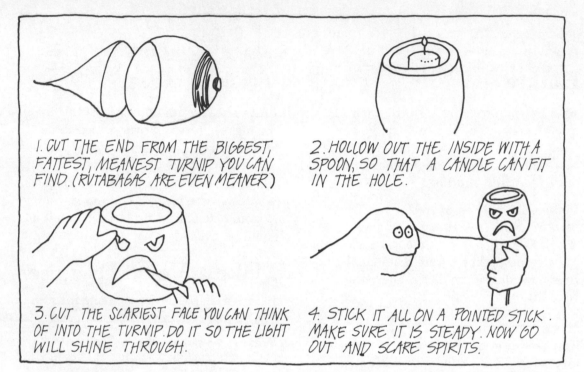

1. CUT THE END FROM THE BIGGEST, FATTEST, MEANEST TURNIP YOU CAN FIND. (RUTABAGAS ARE EVEN MEANER.)

2. HOLLOW OUT THE INSIDE WITH A SPOON, SO THAT A CANDLE CAN FIT IN THE HOLE.

3. CUT THE SCARIEST FACE YOU CAN THINK OF INTO THE TURNIP. DO IT SO THE LIGHT WILL SHINE THROUGH.

4. STICK IT ALL ON A POINTED STICK. MAKE SURE IT IS STEADY. NOW GO OUT AND SCARE SPIRITS.

Legend of Irish Jack

There once was a mean and ornery man called Irish Jack. For a long time he had been pursued by the devil, who wanted his soul.

Now Jack was clever as well as mean. One day he succeeded in tricking the devil into climbing a tree.

Quick as he could, he made a cross on the trunk, so the devil couldn't come down. The devil screamed and begged to come down.

Jack laughed and said that although the devil was in a rather embarrassing predica-

ment, Jack didn't know what he could do to help. Unless, of course, the devil was willing to make a deal.

The deal was that the devil promise never to take Jack's soul. Jack removed the cross when the devil agreed and the two went their separate ways.

Years later Irish Jack died and he found himself at the gates of heaven. But he wasn't allowed through, because he had been so mean and downright ornery. Having no choice, Jack went down to hell.

The devil met him with a grin and said, "Jack, have you forgotten the promise? I couldn't take your soul even if I wanted it."

Irish Jack, continued

With that the devil threw a hot coal at Jack.

Now Jack at the time was munching a wurzel (turnip, to us). As he turned to leave, he caught the coal. Since that time Jack has roamed the earth in search of a place to stay, with the coal in the turnip lighting his way.

To this day, in memory of Jack, a pumpkin with a light in it is called a jack-o'-lantern.

Save the Seeds

When you clean your pumpkin, don't forget to save the seeds to roast.

Wash them, then spread them on a cookie sheet. Put them in an oven at 300° and turn them a few times until they are toasted. Add salt.

Get them while they're hot!

Divinations

Apple Appeal

Peel an apple so the skin is a long, continuous piece. Drop it over your left shoulder. It will form the first initial of your future betrothed.

Key to Your Future

Put a key into a bowl of water. Pour hot wax through the hole in the top. To make the charm work it should be a person's front door key.

Someone with insight — or lots of imagination — should read what the wax shapes mean. For instance, a knife shape would mean that you will be a great surgeon, or a butcher.

Three Luggies

Place three dishes on a table, one of water, one of ink, and one with nothing in it. An unmarried girl who wishes to know about her future mate is asked to choose a plate. If she chooses the dish of water, her husband will be handsome. If she chooses the ink, her husband will be a widower. If she picks the empty dish, she will never marry.

BIG TIME

Insight into Hindsight

The earliest people probably didn't think about the past much. They certainly had no reason to think that the past was any different from the present.

Later, many peoples tried to guess the earth's age. One Chinese legend said the earth was 18,000 years old.

Not until people began to consider the earth in a more scientific way did any idea of the immensity of the past emerge. The concept of *then*, as we think of it now, was invented around 1750 A.D.

In that year Georges Le Clerc, a French gentleman scientist, tried a practical approach to finding out the earth's age. He heated spheres of earth materials and timed their cooling process. He pronounced the earth to be 74,832 years old. His was a step in the right direction.

The first real breakthrough in determining the earth's age came when James Hutton, a nineteenth century Scottish physician and farmer, observed that the surface layers of earth could be a clue to its age.

He said, "The past history of our globe must be explained by what is seen to be happening now."

What he saw was the forces of wind, water, and weather at work on the land. He knew it took a very long time for a river to cut out a valley. So the wearing down process of the elements, which is infinitely slow to human eyes, must mean that the earth has been weathering for many years.

William Smith, an English surveyor of Hutton's time, looked at a lot of ground in his work. He began to notice that layers of rock he studied matched those in other areas. He got the idea that these rock layers could be read like a book.

Charles Darwin and Lord Kelvin added supporting evidence to these ideas. Later, radioactive dating provided proof that the earth's past is indeed vast.

We now estimate the earth to have been born about 4,500 million years ago. That's also known as four and a half billion years.

Written in Rock

Smith's idea of reading rocks like a book is a simple one. The rocks on the surface of the earth are in layers, sort of like a lot of rugs piled one on top of another. So the top rug is the one put down last, right?

It is the same with rocks; the top layer is the newest one. The layers (or *strata*) are in a time order with the oldest one on the bottom.

Sometimes you can see these rock layers along a river bed or highway. Often the layers will be rippled or turned in odd directions due to tremendous internal pressures.

Big Time Line

Four and a half billion is a very big number. That's a lot of earth trips around the sun. It's also a very long time. Certainly too long a time for a human mind to understand.

Big numbers tend to sound alike — billion, trillion, zillion. You know they are big, and each one is bigger than the one before, but it's hard to understand just how big.

Here is the "Big Time Line" to help you understand just how big earth time is.

HERE'S HOW: YOU NEED A PENCIL, SCISSORS, AND PAPER (8½"×11" WILL BE FINE.)

1. FOLD THE SHEET IN HALF LENGTHWISE.

2. IN HALF AGAIN.

3. IN HALF AGAIN SO YOU HAVE 8 SECTIONS.

4. OPEN IT UP AND MARK ALONG THE FOLDS LIKE THIS.

5. NOW FOLD IT IN HALF CROSSWISE.

6. NOW IN THIRDS TO MAKE 6 SECTIONS.

7. CUT ALONG THE LINES YOU DREW IN PART 4.

EACH FOLDED SECTION EQUALS 100 MILLION YEARS.

200 MILLION YEARS

NOW   100 MILLION YEARS

A HUNDRED MILLION IS A BIG NUMBER. THAT IS 100 × 1 MILLION. EVEN A MILLION IS NOTHING TO SNEEZE AT. SUPPOSE YOU STACKED A MILLION BURGERS ON TOP OF EACH OTHER. LET'S SAY EACH ONE IS 2" THICK. HOW TALL WOULD THE PILE BE?

HERE ARE SOME EVENTS TO PUT ON THE LINE:

IN MILLIONS OF YEARS	
4,500	EARTH IS BORN
3,500	FIRST LIFE
1,900	FIRST OXYGEN IN THE AIR
180	FIRST DINOSAURS
135	FIRST FLOWERS, SNAKES (DINOSAURS DIE)
63	FIRST MAMMALS
$\frac{1}{20}$	FIRST HUMANS (HOMO SAPIENS)

CUT UP YOUR TIME LINE, ONE SECTION FOR THE TIME BEFORE LIFE, ONE FOR LIFE BEFORE MAN. HOW MUCH IS LEFT FOR LIFE SINCE HUMANS?

APPLES

There are almost 10,000 varieties of apples. All of them are kin to the crab apple, which is related to the rose.

The difference came about over many years. Generations of people have grown generations of apple trees, encouraging the big, juicy ones and discarding the seeds from the small, mealy ones. In this way they cultivated the *apple of their eye*.

Become a Connoisseur

Apples grow all year round.

In the old days apples were an autumn fruit. Now, because of quick transport and a lot of tampering with apples' biological clocks, we have apples for all seasons.

Have a look in the supermarket. You can tell the month of the year by looking at the names above the apple bins. All the kinds of apples taste, look, and feel different from each other.

Next time look before you bite. Can you tell the difference between a Granny Smith and an American Mother? One thing is certain, it will take a lot of eating to become an apple expert.

A Graft Story

Growing a plant from a seed is a bit like playing a slot machine.

The baby plant has two parents and will show characteristics of each. The problem is that you can never tell when a winning combination will appear. A tree must grow for years and reach maturity before it will produce fruit. Until then you can't tell if you've been lucky or not.

Because a farmer can't afford to take chances, he uses a short-cut to growing fruit he wants. It's called *grafting*.

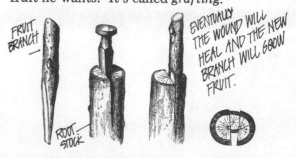

GRAFTING IS A WAY OF JOINING GOOD FRUIT-BEARING BRANCHES TO STRONG ROOT STOCK. THIS WAY, THE FRUIT OF A VERY GOOD TREE CAN GROW FROM MANY TRUNKS.

In Fact

A farmer in West Virginia patiently experimented for years with apple growing and produced nothing but disappointment. Then one of his trees grew big, golden, sweet, juicy fruit.

Word got around quickly and very soon a sharp city nurseryman bought the tree for $5,000.

Moving the tree might have killed it so the nurseryman had an iron cage with a burglar alarm built around the tree. A full-time watchman made sure that no one got their hands on the tree.

From this tree were taken the branches (graft stock) for all the apples today called *golden delicious*.

Apple People Puppets

BECAUSE AN APPLE IS 5/6 WATER YOU CAN, WITH A BIT OF CARVING AND SOME EVAPORATING, TURN AN ORDINARY APPLE INTO A WEIRD, WRINKLED PUPPET PERSON.

START WITH THE BIGGEST APPLE YOU CAN FIND. PARE AWAY THE SKIN.

HOLLOW OUT THE INSIDE

SEE HOW YOUR APPLE SITS. THEN START CUTTING A FACE WHERE IT SEEMS RIGHT. (THE STEM CAN BE ON THE TOP OR BOTTOM.)

KEEP CUTTING UNTIL YOU GET A FACE YOU LIKE. IF YOU MAKE A MISTAKE EAT IT, AND START AGAIN. MAKE A HAPPY AND SAD FACE.

SOAK THE APPLE IN SALT WATER FOR 30 MINUTES. PUT IT IN A WARM DRY PLACE.

Apple People Continued

DEPENDING ON HOW DRY YOUR DRYING SPOT IS, THE HEAD WILL SHRINK UP SHORTLY. YOU CAN MOLD THE FACE WITH YOUR FINGERS. SOMETIME AFTER THE DRYING HAS BEGUN, ADD EYES, TEETH AND THE NECK. IT'S FINISHED WHEN IT'S HARD AND YOU THINK IT WON'T SHRINK ANYMORE.

PRESS IN SEEDS FOR EYES, RICE FOR TEETH

MAKE A NECK BY PUSHING THE HEAD ONTO A PLASTIC BOTTLE NECK. A CUT-AWAY IVORY LIQUID NECK IS A GOOD SHAPE.

SOME PEOPLE EVEN CARVE HANDS. START WITH BLOCKS OF APPLE. CARVE THEM AND DRY THEM THE SAME WAY.

GLUE ON SOME OLD FRAZZLED YARN HAIR.

TUCK THE BODY INTO THE NECK. SLIDE THE HEAD OVER.

SOCK HAT

CUT OFF TIPS OF OLD GLOVES.

CUT A BODY OUT OF AN OLD T-SHIRT OR OTHER SOFT MATERIAL. MAKE IT BIG ENOUGH TO FIT YOUR HAND. STITCH AROUND THE EDGE.

FOR A SUPERSIMPLE BODY CUT A SECTION OF AN OLD SOCK. CUT OUT HOLES SO YOUR THUMB AND FINGERS CAN BE ARMS.

WINDOW SALAD

Window salad gardens can be started any time of year, but they are an especially good way to help make winter more exciting.

Seeds

TOUGH OUTER COAT
EMBRYO (BABY) PLANT
COTYLEDON (STORED FOOD)

You can think of seeds as space capsules for infant plants. They contain an embryo plant, a food supply to feed the plant until it gets established, a tiny bit of water to keep it alive, and a tough outer coat or coats.

The small plant inside the seed is a tough critter that can brave heat and drought for a long time (sometimes two years or longer), and then come to life when the conditions are right.

The stored food in seeds can provide nourishment for other life forms. Many creatures make a living by interrupting the life of a seed and eating it. Seeds in the shape of beans, corn, rice, and wheat are the main food of most humans in the world.

STALK
EMBRYO PLANT
STORED FOOD
STEM

Bulbs

Bulbs, like tubers, are underground food. Onions are bulbs. They contain stem and leaf tissue with a bud in the center. If you put an onion in water (like in the drawing), you will soon have shiny new green stems sprouting from the top of it.

An onion will grow from a seed, storing food in the bulb section the first year. It is at this time that bulbs are usually harvested. The second year it will produce seeds at the top of its stalks. Then it will die. It is a biennial plant, which means it has a two-year life cycle.

Sprouts to Watch

THE FIRST LEAVES ARE CALLED COTYLEDONS THEY CONTAIN STORED FOOD TO FEED THE PLANT UNTIL THE FOOD MAKING LEAVES APPEAR.

THIS IS A GOOD WAY TO SEE EXACTLY HOW A SEED GROWS. YOU NEED A GLASS, A PAPER TOWEL OR FILTER PAPERS, AND SOME COTTON BALLS.

1. ROLL THE PAPER TO FIT THE GLASS. TRIM OFF THE TOP.

2. PUT THE SEEDS BETWEEN THE GLASS AND THE PAPER. FILL THE CENTER WITH COTTON.

3. PUT IT IN A DIM PLACE AND KEEP IT DAMP. MOVE IT TO THE SUN WHEN THEY SPROUT.

Undercover Sprouts

SPROUTS FROM DARK ENVIRONMENTS ARE MORE TENDER

YOU CAN GROW SPROUTS IN YOUR KITCHEN AND EAT THE RESULTS. YOU NEED AN UNGLAZED DISH (LIKE A NEW FLOWER POT), A STRAINER, A SAUCER, AND SOME BEANS. TRY ALFALFA, MUNG BEANS, LENTILS, OR PEAS. YOU CAN EVEN SPROUT GRAINS LIKE RYE, OR WHEAT.

1. PUT 1/4 CUP DRIED BEANS IN A DISH. SOAK THEM OVERNIGHT IN WATER.

2. RINSE THE POT. PUT IN THE BEANS. COVER WITH A SAUCER. PUT THE POT IN A WARM SPOT.

3. CHECK THE SPROUTS EVERY DAY. THEY SHOULD BE DAMP, NOT WET. IF THEY SMELL SOUR GIVE THEM A GOOD RINSE.

Sprout Machine

HERE IS ANOTHER, NEATER WAY TO SPROUT OFF. IT ALLOWS YOU TO RINSE THE SEEDS WITHOUT USING A STRAINER.

1. IF YOU USE A MASON JAR YOU CAN SAVE THE HOLE CUTTING JOB. JUST REMOVE THE LINER.

2. CUT A HOLE IN THE LID. CUT A PLASTIC OR WIRE MESH CIR- CLE TO FIT THE HOLE.

3. USE THE ABOVE METHOD TO GROW SPROUTS. YOU CAN RINSE THEM WITHOUT REMOVING THE LID.

Germination Sensation

YOU CAN GROW YOUR OWN DELICATE GREENS. BUY MUSTARD OR SALAD CRESS SEEDS FROM THE SEED STORE, AND FOLLOW THE PLANTING DIRECTIONS ON THE PACK; OR GROW THE TOWEL GARDEN BELOW.

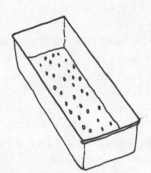  

1. LINE HALF OF AN EGG CARTON OR A TUNA CAN WITH SEVERAL LAYERS OF PAPER TOWELS. SPRINKLE ON THE SEEDS. KEEP IT DAMP AND COVER IT WITH BROWN PAPER.

2. WHEN THE SEEDS HAVE SPROUTED, UNCOVER THEM AND PUT THEM IN A SUNNY PLACE. KEEP THE SPROUTS MOIST.

3. HARVEST THE PLANTS WHEN THEY ARE 2" HIGH. CUT THEM NEAR THE ROOTS. THEY ARE YUMMY ON ROAST BEEF OR CHICKEN SANDWICHES.

Chop Suey

ADD YOUR SPROUTS TO A CAN OF CHOP SUEY OR CHOW MEIN FROM THE SUPER MARKET. HAVE IT WITH RICE AND BREW UP SOME GREEN TEA. EAT THE WHOLE THING WITH CHOP STICKS. IF YOU CAN MANAGE THAT, YOU DESERVE A REWARD. HAVE SOME FORTUNE COOKIES.

Window Salad

YOU CAN TOSS YOUR GREENS INTO A SALAD, OR HAVE THEM ON A CREAM CHEESE SANDWICH. IF YOU ARE VERY SUCCESSFUL WITH SPROUTS, TRY THIS: MIX 1 CUP SPROUTS, A HANDFUL OF SLIVERED ALMONDS, SOME SPRIGS OF CRESS. TOSS IT ALL WITH A DAB OF SOUR CREAM AND A DASH OF GINGER POWDER. SPRINKLE SOME ONION CLIPPINGS ON TOP. MUNCH.

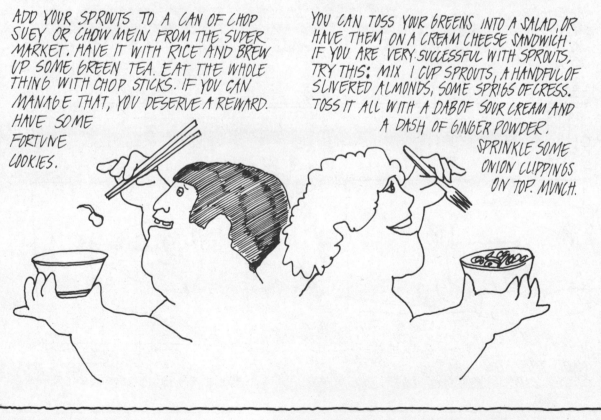

PLANETS

Sun System

Our star is called *sun*. Around it travel nine planets and their thirty-two moons, thousands of asteroids, and billions of comets. All of this mass and motion is called our *solar system*.

Below is a chart for you to draw. It will give you some idea of the planets' places in space. Get some pencils and paper and meet your neighbors!

Planet Words

Planet — comes from the Greek word *planetai*, meaning wanderers.

Planets seem to drift against a background of fixed stars. Actually, all stars are moving also but they are so far away that their movement is hard to detect.

We all know Saturday, Sunday, Monday. Here are some more words with planets in them: jovial, saturnine, mercurial.

Some of the planets were named after Roman gods. Their personalities are clues to what these words mean. You could read Roman mythology to find out about these words. Lazy folks might try a dictionary.

Planet Poster

(or, Interplanetary Travel with a String)

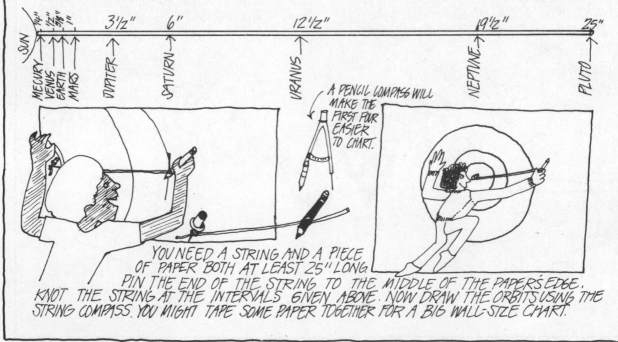

REMEMBER, LIKE ANY CHART THIS IS AN ATTEMPT AT REALITY. THE PLANETS' ORBITS AREN'T EXACTLY ROUND. THEIR MUTUAL ATTRACTIONS PULL THE ORBITS INTO FLATTENED CIRCLES CALLED <u>ELLIPSES</u>. ALSO, EACH PLANET IS MOVING AT A DIFFERENT SPEED, WHICH ISN'T CONSTANT.

¼" ½" ⅝" 1"   3½"   6"   12½"   19½"   25"

SUN MERCURY VENUS EARTH MARS JUPITER SATURN URANUS NEPTUNE PLUTO

A PENCIL COMPASS WILL MAKE THE FIRST FOUR EASIER TO CHART.

YOU NEED A STRING AND A PIECE OF PAPER BOTH AT LEAST 25" LONG.
PIN THE END OF THE STRING TO THE MIDDLE OF THE PAPER'S EDGE.
KNOT THE STRING AT THE INTERVALS GIVEN ABOVE. NOW DRAW THE ORBITS USING THE STRING COMPASS. YOU MIGHT TAPE SOME PAPER TOGETHER FOR A BIG WALL-SIZE CHART.

Sunshine Family

- MERCURY IS SMALL, DENSE AND METALLIC. ONE FACE IS FROZEN, WHILE THE OTHER COOKS IN TEMPERATURES TO 1000°F.

- ALL PLANETS TRAVEL AND SPIN IN A COUNTER-CLOCKWISE DIRECTION, EXCEPT VENUS WHICH MOVES IN CLOCKWISE FASHION. VENUS IS ENCASED IN DENSE CARBON DIOXIDE CLOUDS.

- EARTH IS THE BLUE PLANET. THE LARGEST OF THE INNER PLANETS, IT HAS A DENSE CORE AND A ROCKY CRUST. IT IS COVERED WITH AN OXYGEN NITROGEN ATMOSPHERE. 7/10 OF ITS SURFACE IS WATER.

- MARS., THE RED PLANET, IS THE MOST EARTH LIKE OF OUR SYSTEM. ITS CRATERED SURFACE IS SWEPT BY FIERCE DUST STORMS. IT HAS ICE CAPS, A THIN CARBON DIOXIDE ATMOSPHERE, AND MYSTERIOUS SEASONAL BLOTCHES. THE TEMPERATURE RANGES FROM EARTH WINTER TO DRY ICE.

- JUPITER IS THE GIANT OF THE THE SOLAR SYSTEM. IT IS ONLY A LITTLE DENSER THAN A GLASS OF LEMONADE. THERE IS A MYSTERIOUS "GREAT RED SPOT" ON ITS SURFACE.

- SATURN IS A LIGHTWEIGHT GAS GIANT LIKE JUPITER. IT IS ABOUT AS DENSE AS A MILK SHAKE. LIKE THE SUN AND JUPITER, IT IS MOSTLY HYDROGEN AND HELIUM. THE RINGS ARE ICE FRAGMENTS.

- URANUS IS A LARGE, GREEN PLANET THAT SPINS SIDEWISE. IT IS A VERY COLD 270° BELOW ZERO.

- NEPTUNE, LIKE URANUS, IS A PALE GREEN PLANET WITH A METHANE ATMOSPHERE. ITS TEMPERATURE IS ABOUT 350° BELOW ZERO.

- PLUTO IS PERHAPS A LOST SATELLITE OF NEPTUNE. ITS ORBIT HINTS THERE MAY BE ANOTHER, STILL MORE FAR-FLUNG PLANET.

How to Spot a Planet

You can find four planets fairly easily without a telescope. A planet will appear to have a steadier light than a star.

Once you spot a planet watch it for a few nights in a row. It will move westward with the whole sky. Over the weeks it will change position in relation to the starry background. Can you guess why?

Jupiter

A big, bright planet. In fall, look for Jupiter in the southeastern sky; in winter, in the southwestern sky. With field glasses you can see four of Jupiter's brightest moons. There are twelve of them altogether. The moons will look like bright spots lying to one side of Jupiter in an almost straight line. If you watch for several nights they will change position.

Saturn

Look for it in spring in the southeastern sky; in winter look in the southwestern sky. Saturn will appear bright yellow. Don't expect to see rings unless you have a telescope.

Venus

Venus orbits the sun rapidly and appears to wander in the sky. You will need an almanac to know where and when to find Venus. (You can find an almanac at the library.) The planet is brilliant white and is sometimes far brighter than the other planets. Venus has phases like the moon, which you can observe with a telescope.

Mars

You will need an almanac to help you to know where to look for Mars. Mars shines with a reddish light and moves with great speed.

WINTER

THE TIME OF THE LONGEST NIGHT AND THE
LEAST LIGHT. THE SLOWEST SEASON IN THE
GROWING WORLD. THE FOOD SUPPLY DWINDLES.
IT IS A HARSH TIME FOR CREATURES
IN COLD PLACES. FISH SWIM DEEP INTO
THE WARM UNDER PARTS OF PONDS.
INSECTS VANISH — TO HIBERNATE, OR
WAIT FOR SPRING AS EGGS. EVERY-
THING SLEEPS.

IT LASTS 89 DAYS, 1 HOUR, IT ENDS MARCH

(THE LONGEST NIGHT)

WINTER SOLSTICE — THE

WINTER BEGINS DECEMBER 21. (

FESTIVAL OF LIGHT

Sundown

Since very ancient times, and even still, we light fires to the dying sun around the time of winter solstice.

December 21 is the date of winter solstice. It marks the day the sun is at its low point on its journey across the sky. It is the shortest day of the year and the beginning of our winter. For thousands of years people of many cultures have tried to rekindle the sun, when it reached its lowest ebb, by lighting fires.

Ancient Mesopotamians celebrated the arrival of winter for twelve days with fires, feasting, and gift-giving. Every year their god, Marduk, struggled with the underground monsters of darkness and chaos, and was victorious.

The Jews did, and still do, celebrate Hanukkah, the Festival of Lights.

The Persians lit fires to the god, Mithras.

Romans celebrated the Birthday of the Unconquered Sun and continued feasting with the festival of Saturnalia, a topsy-turvy, anything-goes-type carnival.

Christians celebrate the coming of the Son and call him the Light of the World.

The first Christmas holiday was celebrated at the same time as Saturnalia. It was a calm, spiritual holiday in comparison to the wild Roman celebration.

Christmas is still a festival of light, whether it's in the form of Christmas candles, lights on a tree, or whole cities of electric light during winter darkness.

Christmas Is Late

Our years in western society are numbered from Christmas One.

Before Christians had such a monopoly on western spirits, years were numbered from the founding of Rome.

Not until 533 A.D. was our present system adopted. It was worked out by Dionysus, a Russian monk. It seems he made a mistake in calculating Jesus' birth date.

Herod the Great was king of Judea, where Jesus was born. Herod heard there was a newborn boy that some of the locals were calling king. He decided to do away with the competition. He had all first-born boys between the ages of six months and three years old executed. Herod died shortly after this gruesome deed in the Roman year we would now call 4 B.C. (before Christ). This means, if you think like a detective for just a minute, that Christ was six months to three years old in 4 B.C.

There does seem to be a mistake somewhere . . .

How to Build a Kissing Bough

An old Christmas custom you might like to revive comes from England. It's called making a kissing bough. It was replaced by the Christmas tree around 1850.

The kissing bough is still a nice decoration to look at beside all the other ornaments. It is made from many of the materials we still use when we want to conjure up the spirit of Christmas.

Originally the kissing bough was made from an iron or willow frame, but you can use a coat hanger.

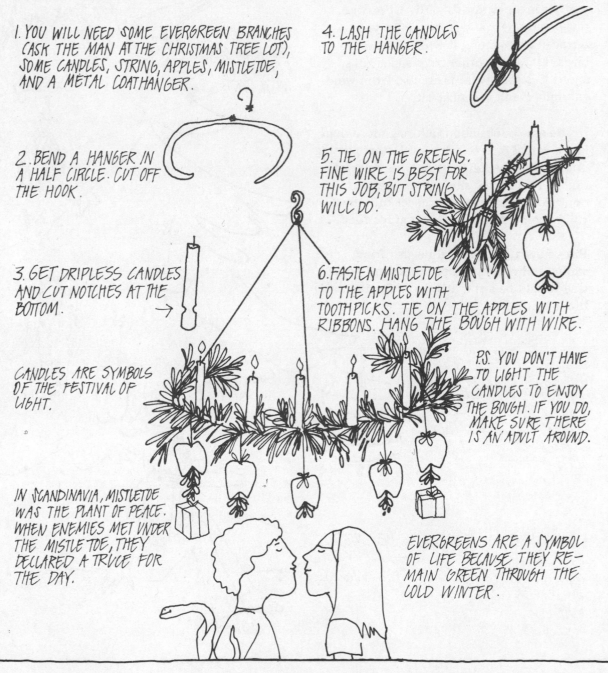

1. YOU WILL NEED SOME EVERGREEN BRANCHES (ASK THE MAN AT THE CHRISTMAS TREE LOT), SOME CANDLES, STRING, APPLES, MISTLETOE, AND A METAL COATHANGER.

2. BEND A HANGER IN A HALF CIRCLE. CUT OFF THE HOOK.

3. GET DRIPLESS CANDLES AND CUT NOTCHES AT THE BOTTOM.

CANDLES ARE SYMBOLS OF THE FESTIVAL OF LIGHT.

IN SCANDINAVIA, MISTLETOE WAS THE PLANT OF PEACE. WHEN ENEMIES MET UNDER THE MISTLE TOE, THEY DECLARED A TRUCE FOR THE DAY.

4. LASH THE CANDLES TO THE HANGER.

5. TIE ON THE GREENS. FINE WIRE IS BEST FOR THIS JOB, BUT STRING WILL DO.

6. FASTEN MISTLETOE TO THE APPLES WITH TOOTHPICKS. TIE ON THE APPLES WITH RIBBONS. HANG THE BOUGH WITH WIRE.

P.S. YOU DON'T HAVE TO LIGHT THE CANDLES TO ENJOY THE BOUGH. IF YOU DO, MAKE SURE THERE IS AN ADULT AROUND.

EVERGREENS ARE A SYMBOL OF LIFE BECAUSE THEY REMAIN GREEN THROUGH THE COLD WINTER.

Christmas for the Birds

Winter is a hungry season for birds.

Here is an old idea from Scandinavia that will make you popular with your feathered friends.

Perhaps you already have a tree in your yard or in a neighbor's yard. Otherwise, put one up near a window, or on your terrace. Remember, it will attract more birds if it is near other trees and shrubs, and if it is somewhat protected from wind and rain — and the local cat.

If you are serious about alluring more than just a casual bird to your yard, start putting out food in the fall, before birds have settled in a wintering site. Once you start, don't forget to keep the feeder full. Birds will become dependent on you for food.

Birds have three survival needs: food, water, and cover. Supply these and your tree should be a star attraction for the bird life in your area.

STRIPS OF BACON RIND FOR YOUR MEAT-EATING BIRD FRIENDS.

FILL A MESH BAG (THE KIND GARLIC COMES IN) WITH SUET.

STRING A DONUT BETWEEN TWO METAL JAR LIDS. PUNCH A HOLE IN THE CENTER OF THE LIDS WITH A NAIL.

SONG BIRDS CAN SOMETIMES BE LURED OUT INTO SIGHT, IF YOU SIT STILL (VERY STILL) AND KISS THE BACK OF YOUR HAND IN A VERY LOUD AND SQUEAKY WAY.

O Christmas Tree

Christmas trees are a rather recent Yule custom. In a way they symbolize the war between early Christians and pagans, or between old and new tradition.

The ancient Germans worshipped in sacred oak groves. According to legend, the missionary, St. Boniface, cut down a pagan oak and, finding a small fir nearby, he substituted it as a symbol for Christians.

While sacred oaks weren't tolerated by Christians, evergreens were acceptable. Probably St. Boniface didn't know that the pagan Romans decorated pines with ribbons and images of their god, Attis.

The moral of this story is, you can't kill custom, though you might manage to change it some.

German immigrants brought the Christmas tree to America in 1830. The first Christmas tree exhibit was held in York, Pennsylvania. Tickets to see it cost 6¼ cents and the money was donated to charity. Christmas conifers have been gaining popularity ever since.

STRING POPCORN, PEANUTS, OR CRANBERRIES.

SPREAD A PINE CONE WITH PEANUT BUTTER, THEN ROLL IT IN BIRDSEED.

CUT OUT SHAPES OF BREAD. USE COOKIE CUTTERS.

TIE ON APPLES, CARROTS, INDIAN CORN, AND OTHER VEGETABLE AND FRUIT GOODIES.

SPRINKLE BIRD SEED ALL AROUND.

BIRD WATCH

North America's bird population is biggest at the end of the summer — when there are an estimated 20 billion birds.

There are considerably fewer birds around in places where it is cold. In the winter birds migrate to places where there is more food (usually south) and where longer days make a longer growing season.

Your feeder might be visited by ten or twenty kinds of birds. An extraordinary number might include forty species of birds. The success of your feeder depends on how attractive you can make it look to birds. If you are on a flight path, migrating birds might have a snack at your feeder on their way north or south.

Bird Blind

Some amateur bird watchers have sighted up to 300 different kinds of birds. An ace observer might see as many as 500 species in a lifetime.

The point is not to become a bird name dropper, but to learn something about birds. You can get closer to the birds who visit your feeder by making a bird blind to fit your window.

If you get very interested in birds, you might want to get a bird identification book to help you. If you have a question about birds that the book can't answer, get in touch with a member of your local bird watching group. Look under *Audubon* in the phone book.

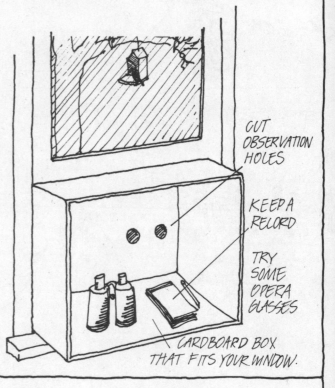

CUT OBSERVATION HOLES

KEEP A RECORD

TRY SOME OPERA GLASSES

CARDBOARD BOX THAT FITS YOUR WINDOW.

Milk Carton Feeder

YOU CAN MAKE A BIRD FEEDER OUT OF A HALF GALLON MILK CARTON. USE IT ALONE OR HANG IT ALONG WITH OTHER BIRD GOODIES ON PAGE 106.

1. CUT AWAY THE SIDE WITH A SHARP KNIFE. CAREFUL!

2. PUNCH A HOLE IN THE TOP. PUT IN A STRING FOR HANGING.

3. PUT IN A PERCH. USE A 1/4" DOWEL, OR AN OLD PENCIL MIGHT WORK.

4. CUT A BASE. IF YOU WANT THE FEEDER TO SIT INSTEAD OF HANG, YOU MIGHT WANT TO PAINT IT.

Guess Who's Coming to Dinner

There are many species of birds. You know that from watching what goes on at your feeder. If you watch closely, you might notice that some birds are very interested in the seed menu, and others like bacon rind and suet.

Birds fall into two fairly definite groups — vegetarians, who are fitted for a diet of seeds and fruit, or nectar-sipping; non-vegetarians, who live on insects, rodents, fish, or food scraps.

An insect eating bird would starve on a berry farm, unless there were insects there. They just don't have the equipment to eat berries. Every creature is equipped to live in a special way, in a particular place. There are some exceptions to this rule. These creatures can be called *generalists*. They can adapt to a wide range of menus and habitats, like humans and flies. Most creatures find a niche where they fit into the scheme of things.

A Dictionary of Parts

You can tell what a bird eats and where it lives just by looking at its mouth and feet.

SEED EATERS HAVE HEAVY, CONICAL BILLS FOR CRACKING.

SPARROWS, JAYS, AND THRUSHES HAVE FEET GOOD FOR PERCHING, HOPPING, AND CLIMBING.

DUCKS HAVE WIDE BILLS FOR SCOOPING AND STRAINING.

SWIMMING BIRDS WEAR WEBS. THE WEBS SPREAD FOR THE POWER STROKE AND FOLD ON THE RECOVERY.

INSECT EATERS SOMETIMES HAVE STRAIGHT BILLS.

PEDESTRIAN BIRDS LIKE CHICKENS HAVE LONG, STRONG TOES FOR STANDING, WALKING, AND SCRATCHING. THE REAR TOE DOESN'T TOUCH THE GROUND.

HAWKS HAVE STRONG, HOOKED BILLS FOR TEARING MEAT.

HAWKS HAVE GRIPPING MEAT HOOK FEET FOR CATCHING AND KILLING.

SHORE BIRDS HAVE LONG, SLENDER BILLS FOR PROBING MUD.

MARSH BIRDS LIKE HERON, HAVE LONG TRIM TOES, WHICH KEEP THEM FROM SINKING IN THE MUD.

OLD ORANGE

This is a very famous tree. It might be related to the oranges sitting in your fruit bowl.

In 1873 Mrs. Eliza Tibbits decided that she would plant oranges in Riverside, California. She visited the United States Department of Agriculture in Washington, D.C. They gave her two small trees newly imported from Brazil. Branches from these trees were later grafted onto other root stock. They began the first navel orange groves in California.

Some of these branches still grow oranges. The old orange tree in the picture still stands in Riverside. It has lived a fruitful life for more than 100 years.

Modern transportation has given us oranges to eat, squeeze, and gulp almost any time we like.

It wasn't always so.

Oranges, until not long ago, were considered a rare treat by most people. At one time rich people might have had their portraits painted holding an orange. Oranges were considered proper refreshment for fashionable folks attending the theater. A proper lady would bite a hole in one end of an orange and daintily suck the juice.

Oranges are probably native to Southern China. The Arabs brought them to South Africa and Spain. The Portugese imported a sweet variety from India. The Spanish brought both kinds to Florida and California.

An Orange in Any Language

The sanskrit word for orange tree is *naranga*. From it comes the Persian word for orange, *naranj*.

In Spanish an orange is called *naranja*; in Portugese, *laranja*; in Italian, *arancia*; in Old French, *arenge* (similar to the Latin word, *aurum*, meaning gold); and in Old English, *orenge*.

Citrus Tricks

Stick Shift Orange

THE NEXT TIME YOU HAVE YOUR FRIENDS OVER AFTER SCHOOL, WHEN IT'S HOT AND YOU'RE OUT OF SODA POP, TRY THIS TREAT. IT JUST MIGHT HIT THE SPOT.

THE HOLLOW KIND

1. YOU NEED AN ORANGE AND A PEPPERMINT STICK. GIVE THE ORANGE A ONCE OVER TO MAKE SURE IT IS JUICY.

2. POKE A HOLE IN THE ORANGE, THEN PUSH IN THE STICK.

KUMQUATS?

3. SUCK AWAY. YOU COULD ALSO TRY LEMONS, TANGERINES, TANGELOS, GRAPEFRUITS, AND KUMQUATS.

Fruit Skin Sculpture

BACK IN THE OLD DAYS, ORANGES WERE PRETTY FANCY FOOD. HERE ARE SOME PRETTY FANCY WAYS TO FIX THEM, FROM A COOKBOOK WRITTEN ABOUT 1650 A.D.

YOU CAN DO YOUR OWN PEEL CARVING WITH NOTHING BUT A FINGER NAIL, OR IF YOU WANT MORE COMPLICATED DESIGNS, USE A KNIFE. IF ANYONE ASKS, TELL THEM YOU ARE MAKING ELIZABETHAN FRUIT ART.

Christmas Orange

For many children sixty years or so ago, Christmas meant oranges in your stocking.

What kind of present was that? Well, if you hardly ever saw one, an orange was pretty magical.

Here are some things to do any time of the year you have an orange. They would also make good gifts if you get stuck for ideas at Christmas time.

Save your orange seeds to plant.

Fruit Dish

You can make nifty dishes from citrus rinds. Use oranges, grapefruits, or lemons. The ones with thick skins are best.

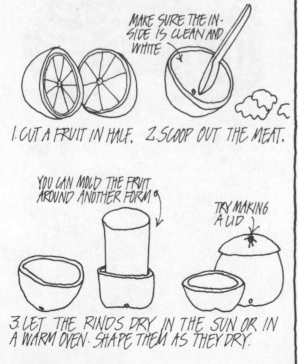

MAKE SURE THE INSIDE IS CLEAN AND WHITE

1. CUT A FRUIT IN HALF. 2. SCOOP OUT THE MEAT.

YOU CAN MOLD THE FRUIT AROUND ANOTHER FORM

TRY MAKING A LID

3. LET THE RINDS DRY IN THE SUN OR IN A WARM OVEN. SHAPE THEM AS THEY DRY.

Armored Orange

In medieval days people wore a hollow ball of gold or silver called a *pomander*. They filled it with sweet smelling herbs and things and put it around their necks to ward off sicknesses.

You can make a more modern version of a pomander with an orange and about half an ounce of whole cloves. Hang it in your closet to ward off the smell of dirty socks.

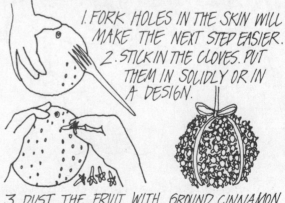

1. FORK HOLES IN THE SKIN WILL MAKE THE NEXT STEP EASIER.
2. STICK IN THE CLOVES. PUT THEM IN SOLIDLY OR IN A DESIGN.

3. DUST THE FRUIT WITH GROUND CINNAMON.
4. HANG IT FROM A RIBBON.

Marvelous Marmalade

This is a good surprise gift for old Uncle Arnie-who-you-never-know-what-to-get-for-Christmas. Everybody likes marmalade. Well, almost everybody.

TO MAKE MARMALADE YOU WILL NEED:

pectin - is the stuff that makes jelly jell. It is a starch found in citrus seeds and the white underskin of citrus fruits. When it's cooked with acid and sugar it will swell up, making your marmalade thick.

1 LARGE ORANGE
2 SMALL LEMONS
4 CUPS SUGAR
4 JELLY GLASSES

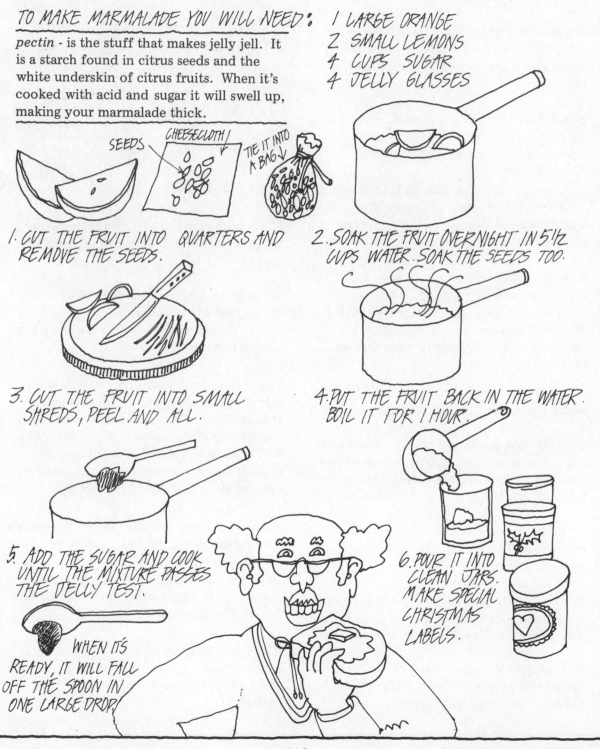

SEEDS   CHEESECLOTH   TIE IT INTO A BAG

1. CUT THE FRUIT INTO QUARTERS AND REMOVE THE SEEDS.

2. SOAK THE FRUIT OVERNIGHT IN 5 1/2 CUPS WATER. SOAK THE SEEDS TOO.

3. CUT THE FRUIT INTO SMALL SHREDS, PEEL AND ALL.

4. PUT THE FRUIT BACK IN THE WATER. BOIL IT FOR 1 HOUR.

5. ADD THE SUGAR AND COOK UNTIL THE MIXTURE PASSES THE JELLY TEST.

WHEN IT'S READY, IT WILL FALL OFF THE SPOON IN ONE LARGE DROP.

6. POUR IT INTO CLEAN JARS. MAKE SPECIAL CHRISTMAS LABELS.

113

SEE STARS

Star Trek

Star watching can be a bit boring, unless you know something about stars.

If you know which stars are ancient, which are young, and where new stars are being born, you'll see the sky in a whole new light.

Some stars are yellow and small, some are gargantuan red, some are blue-white monsters, and some are white-hot dwarfs.

You might know that the starlight reaching your eyes left its stars eons ago. Star watchers know that on a clear night you can see the sky move.

Pull up a chair and watch the stars trek. Sit out on a starry night and place your head against something stationary. Pick a star close to a wall or a pole. Watch the earth turn. The sky moves by at around 800 m.p.h.

Some Hints for City Star Watchers

You can take advantage of some star watching tricks used by early astronomers — before Dutch Trunks (telescopes) were invented.

1. Sit in the dark for 45 minutes before observing. This will adjust your eyes to seeing in dim light.

2. Observe from a room with a tiny opening, to shut out most of the sky brightness. You might leave a slit open in the curtains.

3. Look out the sides of your eyes for the fainter star groups. Your *peripheral* (side) vision is very sensitive at night.

Earth Eyes

Many problems must be overcome before we earth folk can understand the stuff of space.

There is the position problem. We can see the big *out there* from only one place — earth. We are earthbound, or we had been till not long ago.

This means we see stars only as points of light from far-off space. (Which is just as well considering stars are tremendous masses of burning gasses.) To us the Milky Way looks like a stream instead of a lake, and the moon has only one face — until we look at space from another place.

Then there is the twinkle barrier, the earth's atmosphere, which acts as a sort of protective skin for earth life. This makes it difficult to see starlight. Most starlight is steady, but we see it as a flashing phenomenon because of earth's airborne dust.

There is the distance problem. How far is a star? How bright? How much light does it emit? The latter is a problem of great magnitude.

Magnitude

The brightness of a star, its magnitude, can be determined in two ways: how bright it seems, and how bright it actually is.

A very bright star at a greater distance will seem as bright as a weaker, but closer star.

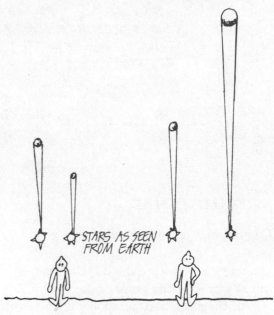

STARS AS SEEN FROM EARTH

The best time to watch stars is on a clear night. This is no easy trick if you live in a haze-covered city.

There is another problem involved in city star-watching that you might never have considered.

Cities are well-lit places. If you have flown over a big city at night or driven from the countryside into an urban area at night, you probably noticed that cities light up the country for miles around. All that light is a big distraction if you are trying to see stars.

When you visit the country, don't forget to bring along your star-watching equipment. Also, have a look at the night. It will be big, black, and pretty impressive.

Star Light - How Bright?

HERE IS A DEVICE FOR MEASURING THE ACTUAL MAGNITUDE OF STARS, IN A ROUGH WAY. IT CAN BE MADE WITH CARDBOARD AND CLEAR CELLOPHANE.

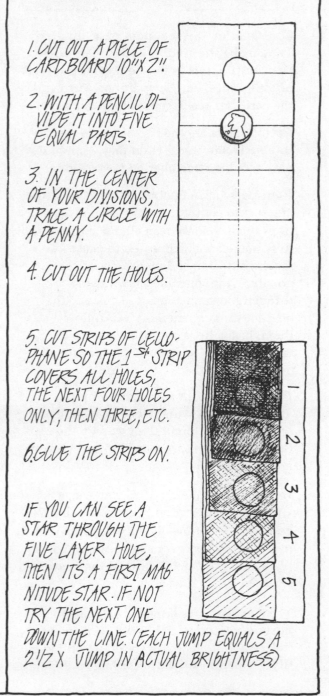

1. CUT OUT A PIECE OF CARDBOARD 10" X 2".

2. WITH A PENCIL DIVIDE IT INTO FIVE EQUAL PARTS.

3. IN THE CENTER OF YOUR DIVISIONS, TRACE A CIRCLE WITH A PENNY.

4. CUT OUT THE HOLES.

5. CUT STRIPS OF CELLOPHANE SO THE 1st STRIP COVERS ALL HOLES, THE NEXT FOUR HOLES ONLY, THEN THREE, ETC.

6. GLUE THE STRIPS ON.

IF YOU CAN SEE A STAR THROUGH THE FIVE LAYER HOLE, THEN ITS A FIRST MAGNITUDE STAR. IF NOT TRY THE NEXT ONE DOWN THE LINE. (EACH JUMP EQUALS A 2½ X JUMP IN ACTUAL BRIGHTNESS)

Constellations

THE BIG DIPPER NOW.
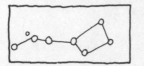

HOW IT WILL LOOK FROM EARTH IN 1000 YEARS.
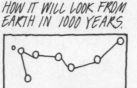

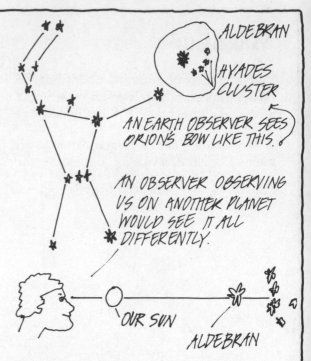

AN EARTH OBSERVER SEES ORION'S BOW LIKE THIS.

AN OBSERVER OBSERVING US ON ANOTHER PLANET WOULD SEE IT ALL DIFFERENTLY.

OUR SUN

ALDEBRAN

ALDEBRAN

HYADES CLUSTER

Constellations are a system of seeing stars. They make star-finding easier. The positions of the stars as we see them are a result of two things, our viewpoint on earth and the earth's place in space at a given time.

Astronomers use the constellation system to help locate stars. Even they sometimes have trouble remembering the patterns.

John Herschel, a famous astronomer of the nineteenth century, said: "The constellations seem to have been almost purposefully named and delineated to cause as much confusion and inconvenience as possible. Innumerable snakes twine through long and contorted areas of the heaven where no memory can follow them; bears, lions and fishes small and large, northern and southern, confuse all nomenclature."

Our constellations were named by the ancients of the Mediterranean, who, being seafaring folk, found their way by the stars. Some star names are Greek or Latin; many are Arabic.

In 140 A.D. Ptolemy of Alexandria, a Greco-Roman astronomer, wrote the *Almagest*. It was a heavenly encyclopedia that named forty-eight constellations and explained in great detail how all the heavens whizzed round the earth.

The *Almagest* was accepted as truth for thirteen centuries. While we have a new theory about planetary travel, we still identify the constellations according to Ptolemy.

Circumpolar

Circumpolar means around the pole.

Circumpolar stars are the ones located in our sky around the poles of the earth. The rest of the stars seen in our sky change with the seasons. Different constellations become visible. Each night the constellations rise in the sky four minutes earlier than the night before. After a year they return to their original positions.

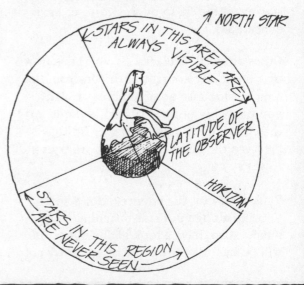

NORTH STAR

STARS IN THIS AREA ARE ALWAYS VISIBLE

LATITUDE OF THE OBSERVER

HORIZON

STARS IN THIS REGION ARE NEVER SEEN

Sky Map

This is a sky map that is good for any night of the year. It is a star chart of the circumpolar stars. Use it outside on a clear night. You might want to take a flashlight along so you can read it. Dim the light with a sheet of colored cellophane so its brightness doesn't interfere with your star watch.

Name some of the brighter stars. If you get really interested you will want to buy a star finder from a nature-bookshop. It will give you names of all the stars on a wheel to turn for the right season. The brightest stars are in the winter sky.

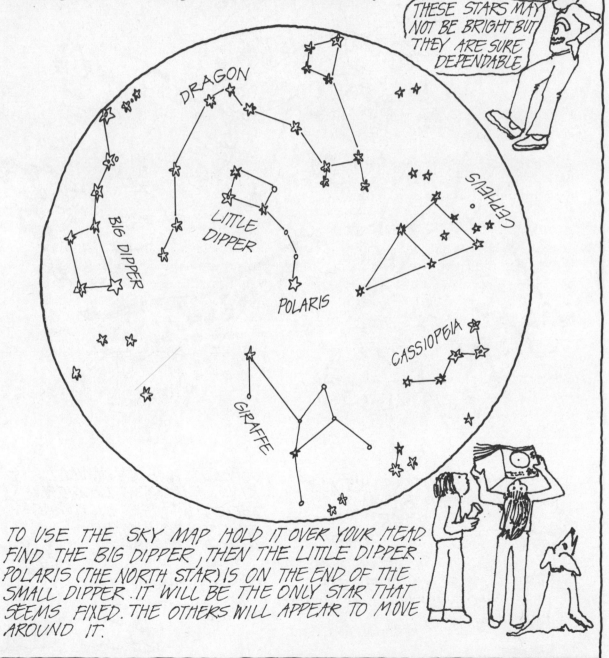

THESE STARS MAY NOT BE BRIGHT BUT THEY ARE SURE DEPENDABLE

DRAGON

BIG DIPPER

LITTLE DIPPER

POLARIS

CEPHEUS

CASSIOPEIA

GIRAFFE

TO USE THE SKY MAP HOLD IT OVER YOUR HEAD. FIND THE BIG DIPPER, THEN THE LITTLE DIPPER. POLARIS (THE NORTH STAR) IS ON THE END OF THE SMALL DIPPER. IT WILL BE THE ONLY STAR THAT SEEMS FIXED. THE OTHERS WILL APPEAR TO MOVE AROUND IT.

What the Ancients Saw

This is a constellation chart for the circumpolar stars. Trace it onto a sheet of transparent paper. Lay it over the sky map on the previous page. It will help you put the stars in groups in case your imagination fails you.

THE DIPPERS ARE ALSO CALLED BIG AND LITTLE BEAR. DRACO IS A DRAGON WITH THE FOUR STAR FACE. HIS OTHER STARS ARE RATHER DIM. GIRAFFE IS ALSO DIM.

CEPHEUS WAS AN ANCIENT KING MARRIED TO CASSIOPEIA. (THEIR DAUGHTER ANDROMEDA RAN OFF TO ANOTHER PART OF THE SKY.)

I'D RATHER WATCH T.V.

Dictionary of Heavenly Bodies

Asteroid - a bit of cosmic debris. There is an asteroid belt, a band of orbiting chunks, between Mars and Jupiter. Diameters of asteroids are from a few miles to several hundred.

Comet - a cosmic tramp. A mass of frozen gasses and dust that may take several million earth years to orbit the sun. It has a tail of glowing gas as it approaches the sun.

Constellation - a group of bright stars which, to some human eyes, makes a pattern in the sky.

Galaxy - is a large group of stars and planets isolated in space from other such groups. Our local galaxy is the Milky Way. It contains billions of stars and even more planets. It is about 100,000 light years wide.

Meteor - a small particle passing through space. Called a falling star when it passes through the earth's atmosphere.

Moon - a smaller body orbiting a planet.

Nebula - this used to be a word that meant galaxy. Now it means a hazy cloud of gas and dust within a galaxy.

Planet - a body that orbits a star.

Star - a huge, glowing globe of gas. Seen from earth, stars look like points of light. A normal star's size and temperature can be judged from its color and brightness.

red - the coolest sort of star. It isn't large enough to burn hotter, so it looks rather dim.

yellow - larger and hotter than a red star.

blue - very hot, very bright star.

Odd Stars - besides the normal stars there are some exceptional kinds.

white dwarf - a dying star that has collapsed to planet size. It burns very brightly for its tiny size.

giant - a star fifteen to twenty times the size of our sun, that burns with all the brightness of at least one hundred suns.

super giant - a star billions of miles in diameter that burns 50,000 times brighter than our sun.

pulsating star - a star which expands and shrinks periodically.

nova - a star which explodes mildly. The star isn't damaged much (a cosmic burp).

super nova - a super explosion. A star's last explosion. A super nova might release as much energy in twenty-four hours as our sun would in a billion years.

Sun - our local star. As stars go, it is a rather ordinary middle-aged, medium-sized yellow star.

Star Words

Here are two words that come from the Latin word *sidus*, meaning "star."

consider - from *considero*, meaning to resolve a problem in terms of the stars; to consult the stars.

desire - from *desidero*, meaning originally to note the absence of stars; to miss or regret.

GROUNDHOG DAY

People have always been trying to figure out the cosmos. Groundhog Day is an attempt at making the earth's cycles more comprehensible. You could say that groundhog theory is based on natural law, except that it seems to be only about thirty percent accurate.

Hog Watchers

Groundhog Day is a substitute for what used to be Badger Day. It was celebrated in Germany. When the Germans settled in Pennsylvania they brought Badger Day with them. Lacking badgers here, they substituted a local animal; thus American Groundhog Day was born.

The Punxutawney Groundhog Club in Pennsylvania has been watching the groundhogs on Gobbler's Knob since 1898. Its rival in the groundhog observing business is the Slumbering Groundhog Lodge of Quarryville, Pennsylvania, which has been observing February 2 since 1908. They watch groundhogs at Octororo Creek and claim that they are ninety percent accurate.

To prevent Pennsylvania from having a groundhog monopoly, Wisconsin has its own Sun Prairie Groundhog Club. The Pennsylvania club members insist that the Wisconsin animal is a prairie dog. The Wisconsin members say, "There's so much coal dust in Pennsylvania, you can't tell a shadow from a smudge."

On the other hand, one weatherman groundhog watcher said that the groundhog was right only twenty-eight percent of the time in sixty years.

Groundhog Theory

A groundhog comes out of hibernation on February 2. If it's cloudy, all is well, winter is at an end. But if the groundhog sees its shadow and it is afraid, it jumps back into its hole. That's a sure sign winter will continue for six more weeks and a smart farmer will wait to sow his crops.

A Natural Law Just Is

Laws are human inventions. Human beings have been trying to crack the secrets of the universe for a long time, so we make up laws that try to explain the patterns of what is.

A natural law comes about as the result of observation. If you see something that always seems to happen, you put it into a theory. Then you test the theory. If it always happens, you can call it a law.

Scientists are clever people who have a knack for looking, then putting their observations into theories. Then they dream up methods to test their theories. They are masters of clever methods and clear thinking.

The Amazing Spin Dry Experiment

Here is a phenomenon to explore. You probably already know that if you spin an object, even a liquid, fast enough, it seems to defy the laws of gravity. Actually, by spinning it you are placing a force on it that is greater than its weight due to gravity. So the liquid remains squashed at the bottom of the container, even though the bottom's up, as long as it's spinning fast enough.

Now see how slow you can go and still remain dry. Have a friend time you in turns-per-ten-seconds. Make sure you are spinning at a constant rate. Make a knot to mark your grip on the string. Now repeat the experiment with a string half as long. Then half that length string. Repeat. And so on.

Is there any relation between the length of the string and how fast you have to spin the bucket? Make a guess. Use the results of your experiment to check it. You are now a member of the scientific community. Try to make up a theory that's not all wet.

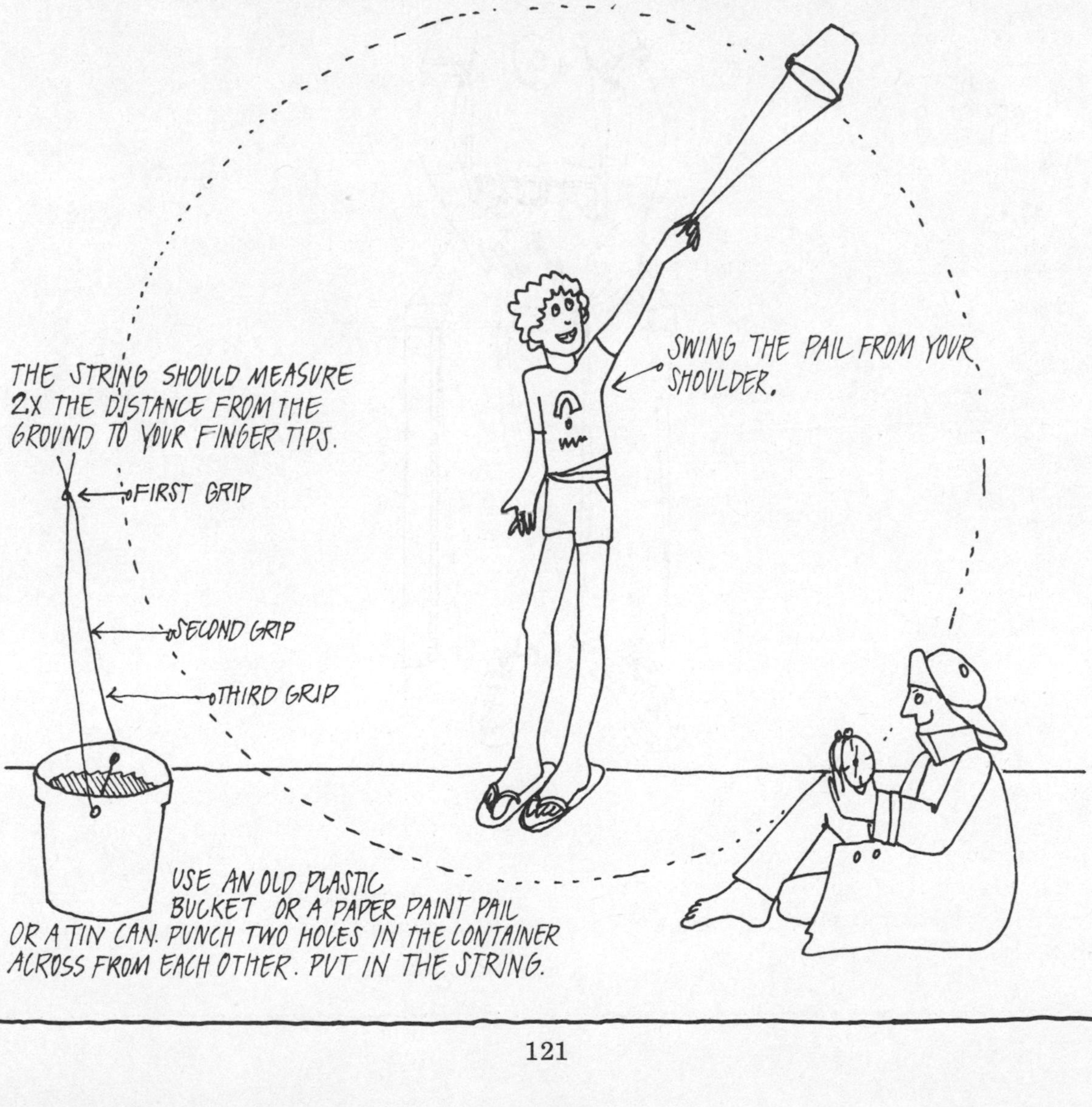

THE STRING SHOULD MEASURE
2X THE DISTANCE FROM THE
GROUND TO YOUR FINGER TIPS.

← FIRST GRIP

← SECOND GRIP

← THIRD GRIP

SWING THE PAIL FROM YOUR SHOULDER.

USE AN OLD PLASTIC
BUCKET OR A PAPER PAINT PAIL
OR A TIN CAN. PUNCH TWO HOLES IN THE CONTAINER
ACROSS FROM EACH OTHER. PUT IN THE STRING.

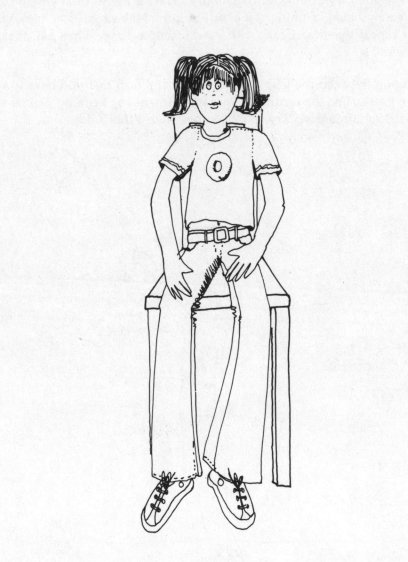

WE HAVE COME TO THE END OF ONE EARTH
TRIP ROUND THE SUN.
THE CYCLE BEGINS AGAIN.
THE SAME OLD TRIP? WELL, NOT EXACTLY.
FOR ONE THING, THE SEASONS NEVER
SEEM TO RUN THE SAME WAY TWICE.
THERE MIGHT BE AN EARLY SPRING OR
HARDLY A FALL AT ALL. NOT TO MENTION
A BIG TIME CHANGE LIKE A LONG DRY
SPELL OR AN APPROACHING ICE AGE.
THERE IS EVIDENCE THAT SHOWS THE
EARTH MAY BE SLOWING ON ITS ANNUAL
CIRCUM-SOLAR FLIGHT, SO THE SEASONS
WILL CHANGE A LITTLE SLOWER.
SO AT BEST, YOU CAN EXPECT THINGS TO
BE FOREVER REARRANGING AND CONSTANTLY
CHANGING.
THE UNIVERSE NEVER RESTS.

THE END

(AND THE BEGINNING)